ART
AND
DESIGN

Philip Carlo Paratore

The University of Maine at Augusta

PRENTICE-HALL, INC.
Englewood Cliffs, New Jersey 07632

Library of Congress Cataloging in Publication Data

PARATORE, PHILIP CARLO
  Art and design.

  1. Design—Philosophy. I. Title.
NK1505.P34 1985   745.4'01   84-8435
ISBN 0-13-046541-0

Editorial/production supervision: Virginia Rubens
Cover design: Celine Brandes, Photo Plus Art
Interior design: Philip C. Paratore
Manufacturing buyer: Harry P. Baisley
Page layout: Peggy Finnerty

© 1985 by Prentice-Hall, Inc., Englewood Cliffs, New Jersey 07632

Printed in the United States of America

10 9 8 7 6 5 4 3 2 1

For my wife, Tina Marie

0-13-046541-0   01

PRENTICE-HALL INTERNATIONAL, INC., *London*
PRENTICE-HALL OF AUSTRALIA PTY. LIMITED, *Sydney*
EDITORA PRENTICE-HALL DO BRASIL, LTDA., *Rio de Janeiro*
PRENTICE-HALL CANADA INC., *Toronto*
PRENTICE-HALL OF INDIA PRIVATE LIMITED, *New Delhi*
PRENTICE-HALL OF JAPAN, INC., *Tokyo*
PRENTICE-HALL OF SOUTHEAST ASIA PTE. LTD., *Singapore*
WHITEHALL BOOKS LIMITED, *Wellington, New Zealand*

CONTENTS

Part III: Dominance Factors   57

Part IV: Applications

Part V: Major Matrixes

PREFACE

Art and Design is a book for anyone who is curious about what design is and how it works. It is for the craftsman, the critic and the connoisseur, the Sunday painter and the serious artist. It is for the art lover, the art teacher and, most of all, the art student.

Art and Design has two major goals: (1) to present a comprehensive, interdisciplinary overview of design; (2) to provide essential information for students enrolled in foundations courses in art programs. Let's briefly discuss these goals.

Design comes in an almost infinite number and variety of forms. It is present on virtually every level of life, from the submicroscopic world of atoms to the macrocosmic world of interstellar space. It is also present in the floor plan of your home and in the behavioral patterns of animals in the wild. Design is pervasive, profound and commonplace all at once. For this reason, *Art and Design* takes a comprehensive, interdisciplinary approach to design. This approach has some unique advantages: If, for example, the principles of visual design can be shown to have similarities with the principles of organization in animal communities or with the principles of musical harmony, the result is a richer, deeper appreciation and understanding of design as a whole. This is the primary goal of *Art and Design*.

Our second goal focuses on practical information for art students. *Art and Design* provides clear, concise discussions on subjects such as shape, size, space, color, texture, visual perception, optical illusion, balance, tension, and dominance. The writing style is straightforward but provocative, making abundant use of comparisons and analogies. A montage-like format is often used to stimulate the reader's imagination and encourage creative thinking. In *Art and Design,* information is often a point of departure, rather than an end in itself.

Art and Design is unique in its approach to the study of art in several ways. Firstly, it has well-defined goals. These goals and the reasons for them are discussed in detail in the book's introduction. Secondly, *Art and Design* contains a major theme known as "field-event theory," which is developed throughout the text. Field-event theory is presented clearly in simple, well-defined terms at the outset of the book. It provides *Art and Design* with a cohesiveness, unity and sense of direction which is uncommon in contemporary design texts.

A brief acquaintance with field-event theory shows it to be closely related to the experimental figure-ground work of the Gestalt psychologists. However, it greatly expands upon the figure-ground model in order to bridge the gap between abstract theory and practical application to design. In educational jargon, field-event theory may be considered a "learning model" for art students.

The disparity between theory and practice is a common problem in education, particularly for the beginning art student. *Art and Design* tries to show that theory and practice are interdependent parts of the learning experience. It does this by linking together general ideas and specific practices as often as possible, both in the text and in the accompanying illustrations.

Art and Design contains over two hundred line drawings, diagrams, illustrations and photographs. Their primary purpose is to illustrate the various subjects and themes presented in the text. But they have a secondary purpose as well: to challenge the reader to visualize and think creatively. There is a wide variety of photographs of works of art by artists representing many different styles, periods and cultures. Photographs of art often appear adjacent to photographs of people, places, objects, animals, stars and planets, producing an evocative collage of ideas and images. The goal is to convey visually the concept of a broad, comprehensive overview of art and design.

Lastly, *Art and Design* is unique in its concern for effective verbal communication in all facets of the design dialogue. This concern is apparent in Part IV, Applications, which provides a series of semantic and discursive exercises intended to develop the student's ability to discuss design objectively and constructively. It is also apparent in Part V, Major Matrices, which consists of a vocabulary of descriptive terms relevant to design and art crticism in general.

Art and Design is an innovative book with some unorthodox but down-to-earth ideas about what design is and how to teach it. Its aims are high, its themes are tenaciously developed. It is written in the spirit of inquiry and invention that is so vital a part of our cultural heritage. Hopefully, *Art and Design* will be a useful and unique addition to the many fine design texts available today.

ACKNOWLEDGMENTS

Many people have assisted in one way or another to make this book a reality; they all deserve and have my enduring gratitude. Special thanks to Charles Danforth, Joshua Nadel and Robert Katz for their steady moral support and encouragement; Richard Blanchard for his assistance in preparing illustrations; Bruce Armstrong for his help in preparing photographs; Virginia Rubens for her expert handling of the book's production at Prentice-Hall; and Norwell F. Therien, Jr., Executive Editor for Humanities at Prentice-Hall, without whom this book would simply not have come to fruition. Finally, I would like to thank all my colleagues and students at the University of Maine at Augusta for their part in creating an atmosphere in which ideas could flourish and develop into a book like *Art and Design*.

I would like to thank the following authors and publishers for granting me permission to include brief passages from their publications:

RUDOLPH ARNHEIM, *Art and Visual Perception.* University of California Press, Berkeley.

A. H. BECK, *Words and Waves.* Weidenfeld & Nicolson, London.

JACOB BRONOWSKI, *A Sense of the Future.* © 1977, The MIT Press, Cambridge, Mass.

EDMUND CARPENTER, *They Became What They Beheld.* E. P. Dutton, Inc., New York.

T. S. ELIOT, "The Love Song of J. Alfred Prufrock," from *Collected Poems 1909–1962* by T. S. Eliot. Copyright 1936 by Harcourt, Brace, Jovanovich, Inc.; copyright © 1963, 1964 by T. S. Eliot. Reprinted by permission of the publisher.

WALLACE FOWLIE, "Winter Party," from *Rimbaud, Complete Works, Selected Letters.* © 1966, University of Chicago Press.

HUBERT AND MABLE FRINGS, *Animal Communication.* Blaisdell Publishing Company.

MARTIN GARDNER, *The Ambidextrous Universe.* Basic Books, Inc.

JANE GOODALL, *In the Shadow of Man.* Copyright © 1971 by Hugo and Jane van Lawick-Goodall. Reprinted by permission of Houghton Mifflin Company, Boston.

JOHANNES ITTEN, *The Art of Color.* Copyright © 1973 by Otto Maier Verlag. Reprinted by permission of Van Nostrand Reinhold Company, New York.

LAO TSU, "Eleven" and "Forty-Five" from *Tao Te Ching* by Lao Tsu, translated by Gia-Fu-Feng and Jane English. Copyright © 1972 by Gia-Fu-Feng and Jane English. Reprinted by permission of Alfred A. Knopf, Inc.

OTTO LOWENSTEIN, *The Senses.* Penguin Books, Inc., New York.

MARSHALL McLUHAN, *Understanding Media.* © 1964 by McGraw-Hill Book Company, New York. Reprinted with permission.

CONRAD G. MUELLER, MAE RUDOLPH AND THE EDITORS OF TIME-LIFE BOOKS, Life Science Library/ *Light and Vision.* © 1966 Time, Inc., New York.

ARTHUR RIMBAUD, *Illuminations.* Copyright 1946, © 1957 by New Directions Publishing Corporation, New York. Reprinted by permission of New Directions.

MASAOKA SHIKI, *Modern Japanese Haiku: An Anthology.* Ed. Makoto Ueda. © 1976, University of Toronto Press.

OSVALD SIREN, *The Chinese on the Art of Painting.* Reprinted by permission of Schocken Books Inc., New York. Copyright © 1963 by Schocken Books Inc.

COLIN TURNBULL, *Tradition and Change in African Tribal Life.* Reprinted by permission of Harper & Row, Publishers, Inc., New York.

BENJAMIN WHORF, *Language, Thought and Reality.* © 1971, The MIT Press, Cambridge, Mass.

Lastly, I would like to thank the following museums for their assistance in obtaining photographs of works of art in their collections: The Museum of Modern Art, New York; The Metropolitan Museum of Art, New York; The Museum of Fine Arts, Boston; The Isabella Stewart Gardner Museum, Boston; The Art Gallery of Ontario, Toronto, Canada; The National Gallery of Art, Washington, D.C.; Haags Gemeentemuseum, The Hague, The Netherlands. For nature photography: The American Museum of Natural History, New York; the Maine Department of Inland Fisheries and Game, Augusta; the National Park Service, Washington, D.C.; and NASA, Washington, D.C.

Rembrandt van Rijn
Self-Portrait
Andrew W. Mellon Collection
National Gallery of Art, Washington, D.C.

INTRODUCTION

Comprehensive Foundation

The major objective of field-event theory is to establish a comprehensive foundation for the study of design. This foundation should be broad and encompassing, able to adapt to the ever-increasing complexity of our world. It should be resilient, for challenge and change are never far off. And it must be boldly comprehensive, for design is an expression of intelligence and creativity, encompassing a full spectrum of human experience. Field-event theory strives to integrate that experience in a spirit of contemporary inter-disciplinary art education.

A Design Model

Field-event theory is a conceptual model for the study of design. Its approach is simple and consistent. Basic principles are identified and essential terms defined. The application of these principles and terms is explored, not only in art, but in a wide range of academic fields and disciplines. Psychology, physics, philosophy, acoustics, zoology, sociology, music, and design are just a few of the fields to which field-event theory may be applied. It is general and comprehensive, to encourage an interdisciplinary approach, and flexible, to accommodate the process of cross-reference and conceptual bridge-building that is so important a part of its mission. But it is also functional. Field-event theory is a diagnostic tool readily applicable to routine problem-solving in design. In the studio, it helps us to answer the most basic kinds of questions: "What works and why?" Although artistic design problems will never be solved exclusively by quoting principles or stating formulas, it is surely to one's advantage to have a consistent and reliable model to work with. Field-event theory provides this model.

Fragmentation

One of the perennial problems of education is the fragmentary way in which information is classified and structured. Some theorists argue that this is a natural consequence of sheer quantity, citing the "information explosion"; others, that it is a logical extension of the "scientific method." Still others argue that it stems from logic itself. But our major concern is with its impact on creativity: Creativity requires the willingness and ability to *declassify* and restructure information and experience. In this, it is like "magic," not bound by universal laws of behavior: The ordinary may become extraordinary at any moment. Magic is incomprehensible to the modern, literate mind, but, kindly remember, so is most "modern art."

Nature and Culture

Nowhere does modern fragmentation have a more disastrous impact than on the historic relationship between culture and nature. And this fragmentation is no longer confined to a minority of industrialized nations. As so-called "third world" countries embrace the mystique of modern technology and industrialization, they too encounter a disconnected and fragmented universe. The divorce of culture and nature is thought by many to be one of the major dilemmas of the twentieth century. It is about as debilitating to ecology as the separation of mind and body is to philosophy. Yet this is a "new" problem, a few hundred years old at most, for until relatively recent times, nature and culture were intimately connected. There was no cultural progress except by agreement with nature. Indeed, nature gave rise to culture and not the reverse. But today nature sits potted and plotted, criss-crossed by highways and turnpikes, pressed into planters and penthouse gardens. In modern currency, nature is a "zoo" or a "vacation." It is *National Geographic Magazine.* Museums, libraries, concert halls, opera houses, universities, galleries and theaters are hallmarks of culture, and, with rare exceptions, they are segregated from nature. Hanging leafy plants in the museum cafeteria is no solution. We seem to have cast our present in concrete, but the future remains, hopefully, to be formed.

Unity

This is assuredly not a call for a "back to nature" movement, for nostalgia is more of a problem than a solution. It is, rather, a call for the reunion of nature and culture, and ultimately a call for unity itself. Disunity prevails and has for a long time. We live, most of us, in a *multiverse,* not a *universe,* enchanted by what we know but thoroughly bewildered as to how in the world it fits together. Polar bears, computers and paintings are all of one world. And so are John Cage, Jimi Hendrix and Ludwig Von Beethoven; Norman Rockwell, Andy Warhol and Pablo Picasso. We applaud the variety of life, unaware of its unity. The first lesson of ecology is that the world is a whole, that everything on earth is somehow related. But rarely do we see it this way. Rather, we see and study it in bits and pieces; our world seems fleeting and fragmentary, and, often, so do we.

Field-event theory is by no means original or novel in its pursuit of a unified field; it is an ancient quest. But unity itself is only a metaphor. It can never be fully realized, for the world is much too vast and complex. We look to it as we look to a far-distant goal, with hope and a little apprehension. We are willing to travel knowing that we cannot arrive. Unity is a metaphor and, like all metaphors, expresses the proverbial human reach for that which is forever beyond our grasp.

Principles, Patterns, and Laws

Thanks to "media-smart" natural scientists around the world, we are today keenly aware of the structural tightness of the ecological system. The exquisite chain of relations between things on all levels of life is a regenerating source of delight, wonder and wisdom. One hundred million years ago, planet Earth possessed an ecology based on patterns, principles and organic systems that are still in effect today. In the past, our progress has depended on our sensitivity to those principles and patterns, and it is no different today.

Western science has successfully progressed over the centuries because it was able to discover and verify laws of behavior that applied not merely to single objects (or events) but to classes of objects. The premise is that *all* objects of the same class obey the same laws. And, further, that these laws hold equally well any time and any place. From our present perspective, it is easy to see how these notions greatly simplified and accelerated the learning process. Time and space and all they contained were made uniform and predictable. But that was yesterday, when the scientific method, with its stress on observation, seemed to be flawless. Today, our perceptions and presumptions are undergoing a subtle change. We are no longer able to rely on direct observation for all the answers, a realization brought about by modern physics. Verification and the very concept of "proof" are not quite what they used to be. We might say that they have mellowed with age.

Today, we are all in roughly the same position as the subatomic physicist who must accept the fact that his very act of observation influences the behavior of the phenomenon being observed. The symbolic value of his dilemma is immense, for it highlights the perennial problem of knowledge: The observer is the limitation. This simple truth is equally humbling in science and art.

The disparity between "what we see" and "what we know" probably began in earnest with the discovery that the world was round. Although our eyes and our common sense told us it was flat, we learned to think of the world as global, never completely understanding why things didn't simply fall off. We learned about gravity and other mysterious forces that kept our feet on the ground and the water in our oceans. And then we learned that our world was spinning and speeding through space at unbelievable velocities. We learned that the sun was an atomic furnace and that only its immense distance from earth prevented our fiery destruction. We learned that the earth was a tiny speck in the vastness of the universe. Our common sense was appalled. Our sensorium paled. We faced a new world which could no longer be taken for granted.

Meaning

How is meaning shaped in this new, extrasensory world? Relatively. We have learned that many of our most basic, conventional judgments are relative to our point of view or frame of reference. In America, the Far East is synonymous with the Orient; but in Japan, the Far East is probably California. On a much grander scale, the sun is the center of our solar system, but it is on the edge of our galaxy, the Milky Way. In space, things occupy apparently different positions, depending on our frame of reference or field. The same is true of meaning; it is always relative, shaped by the field in which it is perceived.

Meaning emerges from relationships. Nothing exists, or is perceived, in isolation. A design acquires its form and meaning from the relationships on which it is based. In pictorial design, this is called composition; in music, orchestration; in nature, ecology. The process of developing meaning through the organization of relationships is analogous in all fields, in all media and for all artists.

Field-event theory is a model for the comprehensive study of design in the world. Its application is limited only by one's own imagination. But, in the last analysis, theories and models are not ends in themselves; they are a means of discovery and growth and progress. They are there to serve, not to be served. And no theory is fail-safe. Jacob Bronowski puts it aptly: "The man who proposes a theory makes a choice—an imaginative choice—which outstrips the facts." A theory is, it seems, an expression of choice, imagination and, finally, chance. After all, we must all take our . . .

chances!

FIELD-EVENT THEORY

PART I

Design

Design is a statement of order and organization. Its goal is unity. For this reason, the symbolic value of design in humanistic philosophy is clear: it is an expression of man's ubiquitous quest for order.

A design must stand as an organized entity or idea, whether it is a painting, a poem, a sonata or a bridge. It must "hold together." Even the highly charged, emotional works of Van Gogh or Beethoven transcend personal chaos and disorder to achieve plastic organization.

Organization itself comes in an almost infinite number and variety of forms. Birds flying south in formation, systematic erosion of a lake shore, faceted brushstrokes in a Cézanne still life, and the floor plan of the local library are all expressions of order and organization.

Unity

The central goal of design is *unity*. Unity is an expression of organization and order. All systems, designs, plans, patterns, schemes, arrangements, compositions and programs pursue, in some way, the ideal of unity.

Field-Event Theory

Field-event theory holds that there are two general ways in which information is organized to achieve unity:

1. **Fields**
2. **Field-Event Relationships**

Fields

A field consists of a set of characteristics which are uniform in time and space.

A field is a family, a community, a commonality and a concord. An ocean is a field. A meadow is a field. Environments in general are fields. Culture is a field; so is the printed page or a painter's blank canvas. Fields are uniform, homogeneous, integrated, continuous, consistent and constant.

In the figure ground model developed by Gestalt psychologists, the *ground* is the *field*.

Fields are organized on the basis of *harmony*. They consist of elements which are alike, that share the same characteristics and are more or less equal; no part of a field is any more important than any other part. *Fields are non-hierarchical systems of organization.*

Field-Event Relationships

A field-event relationship consists of two sets of characteristics which are differentiated in time and space.

An event is a differentiated element, unit, or individual; a figure, an act or an occurrence. An event may also be described as an *anti-field*.

A field-event relationship is a juxtaposition, a bond, a marriage between two sets of opposing characteristics, a pair of complements and a union of polarities.

An ocean is a field; an island is an event. An ocean and an island together form a field-event relationship. A meadow and a buck form a field-event relationship. A symphony orchestra and its conductor form a field-event relationship. The stroke of the painter's brush on a blank canvas comprises a field-event relationship.

Field-event relationships are organized on the basis of differentiation and contrast. They consist of elements which are "unlike" and are of unequal value. Relationships that contain elements of unequal value exhibit dominance or ranking order. Since dominance is the main feature of hierarchies, a field-event relationship can be considered a hierarchical system of organization.

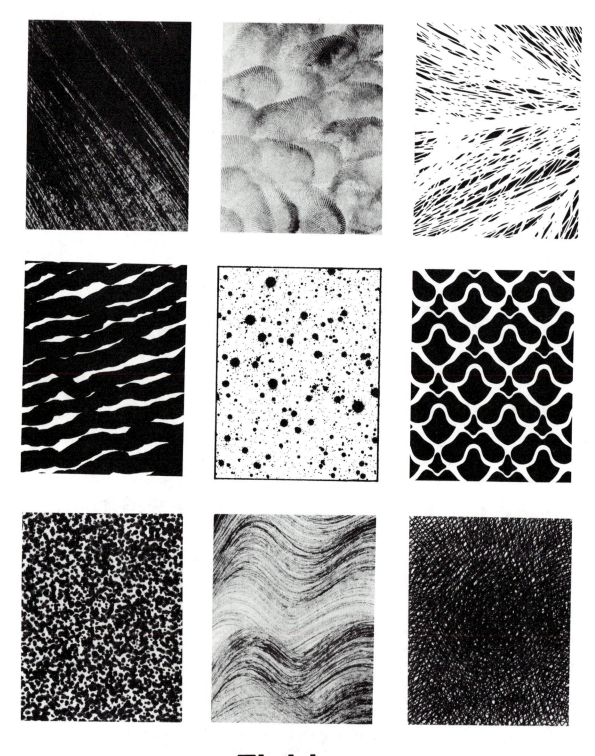

Fields

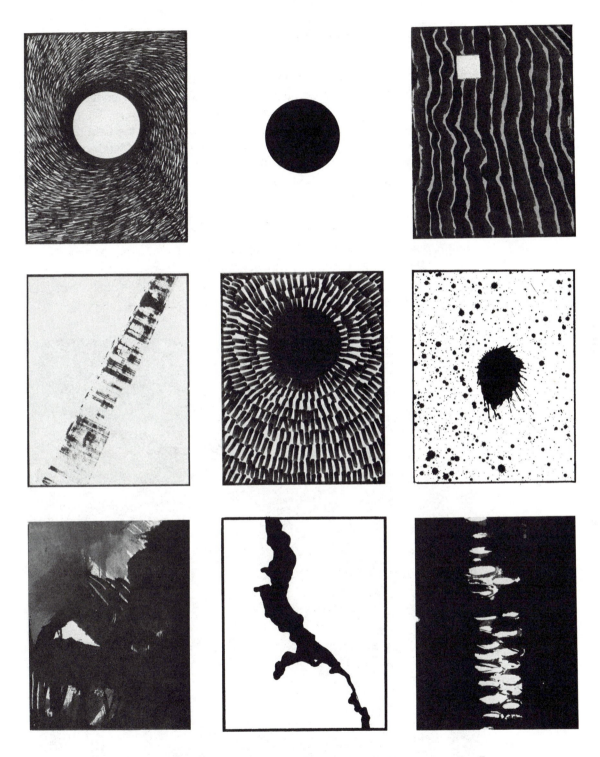

Field-Event Relationships

A Continuum

A visual model of fields and field-event relationships shows them to be conceptual polarities on a theoretical design continuum. The continuum itself graphically symbolizes unity. A central tenet of field-event theory is that designs generally establish an orientation toward either the field polarity or the field-event polarity of this continuum. A painting by Claude Monet, for example, would be considered a field-oriented design, while a painting by Rembrandt would be considered field-event oriented. Both achieve unity, but by vastly different means.

Field-event theory hopes to show that the terms *field* and *field-event relationship* and their polar juxtaposition on a continuum render a model for the organization of information in general, extending beyond design into perception, concepts of meaning, and learning, language, behavior, and structure in both animal and human societies.

Claude Monet
Water Lilies
Oil on canvas. 89.5 × 93.5 cm.
Purchase of Arthur Gordon Tompkins Residuary Fund
Courtesy, Museum of Fine Arts, Boston

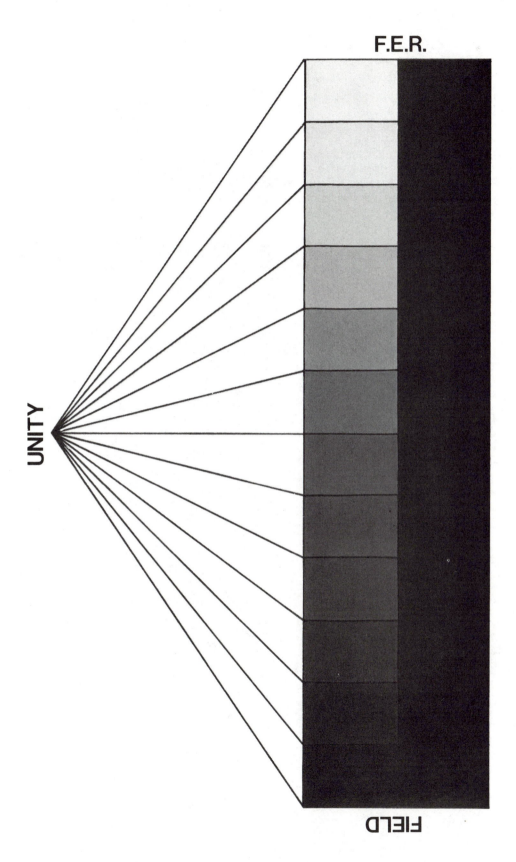

F.E.R.

UNITY

FIELD

DESIGN CONTINUUM

The design continuum illustrates the two polarities of organization, fields and field-event relationships. A series of graduated steps lies between these two poles, suggesting a continuum of organizational options.

PART II

DOMINANCE

 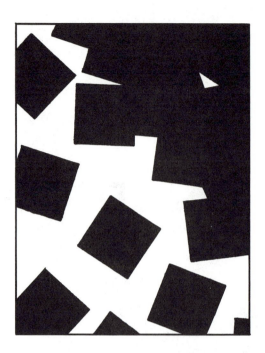

DOMINANCE

Field-Event Relationships and Dominance

Field-event relationships are hierarchical systems of organization. In hierarchies, there is always a ranking-order in which some elements or individuals are more important than others and, consequently, get more attention. Those apparently important elements or individuals are considered to be "dominant." In a typical field-event relationship the event is dominant; the field acts as a "ground" and is generally subordinate in relation to the event. A black bear on a square acre of land is a vividly dominant event. A racoon on an acre of land is considerably less dominant as an event, a mouse is very much less dominant and an ant is not dominant at all. If all four of these creatures occupied the same acre of land, a distinct hierarchy would be immediately established. This hierarchy would be based on dominance and would represent a system of natural order and organization.

Dominance hierarchies are established for the same reason in design and nature. They provide a ranking-order among the various elements or events and, at the same time, help to determine their relative value and meaning.

In a painter's eyes, a bear on an acre of land is graphically comparable to a solid shape on a rectangular field. In both cases, field-event relationships are vividly articulated with strong contrast and well-established dominance.

Dominance is inherent in field-event relationships and in hierarchical systems of organization generally. It appears everywhere, pervading culture and nature alike. But before we delve any further into its application to design, we should spend a little time defining and describing it. Dominance is not quite as simple as it sounds.

What Is Dominance?

Dominance is defined in dictionaries as authority, the power to rule and control. For the average person, it is a term laden with cathexis. Its emotional overtones are apparent to all, especially in an age of intense self-consciousness and self-examination such as ours. But dominance occurs in many forms and is not simply a matter of brute force or overwhelming strength. In both animal and human societies, a less powerful but highly charismatic individual often becomes dominant as a result of his or her **capacity to attract and hold attention.** A dominant figure is likely to be seen not only first but most. Sometimes an unusual combination of characteristics or behaviors will converge in one individual, resulting in a dominant figure. On the social level, it is not uncommon for individuals to form coalitions or relationships which result in dominance due to their combined strength. This has been observed in chimpanzee and baboon troops and is obviously a familiar phenomenon in human societies. In nature, as in culture, dominance is a complex and dynamic system. It is not rigid. It is, rather, highly sensitive to influence and open to change. In this way, it remains responsive to new challenges and conditions, providing the whole—the society or the species—with the flexibility so crucial to survival.

Field-event relationships are essentially expressions of dominance. Events are naturally dominant in their fields: the sun dominates the sky, a mountain dominates the desert. By definition, events oppose fields, and by their opposition, dominate them. This is a fairly simple matter when there is one event in a field, but when there is more than one, the problem becomes much more complex. In such cases, a ranking-order is established in which one top-ranking event is deemed dominant. As the number of events increases, dominance becomes more difficult to establish and hierarchies more cumbersome, resulting in a less efficient system of organization. However, masterworks like Gauguin's *"D'où Venons Nous? Que Sommes Nous? Où Allons Nous?"* and Picasso's *Guernica* show us that complex, hierarchical configurations of field-event relationships are not impossible.

Dominance in Animals

Dominance in animals is purely functional. It is an organizational system which establishes order among individuals and within groups. Wolves, baboons, geese, and gorillas live in societies with a hierarchical structure based on dominance. It is an unhappy and abused animal that does not know its place in this hierarchy. Its very survival is at stake. Dominance in animals is a way of clarifying relationships between individual and individual, individual and group. In essence, it shows how the parts relate to the whole.

Dominance ultimately benefits the group and the species (the whole) by increasing its chances for survival. In a savanna baboon troop of forty members, dominant males occupy the group's center, near the mothers and infants who rely on them for protection. At the group's edge are subordinate, peripheral males. As zoologist Lionel Tiger explains, "The peripheral males—the most expendable—are at the edges, where they are most likely to encounter predators and give the warning." He further explains that "the dominant animal is the one to whom the rest pay the most attention."

Focusing attention on a dominant member—a leader—seems to be a natural consequence of the baboon social system and is critical not only in emergencies but in feeding, moving, mating, raising their young and social rituals of all kinds. Dominance in animals has none of the manipulative, self-serving overtones with which it is associated in human societies. Neither is it magnanimous. It is a simple statement of structure.

Structure in animal societies and structure in design are analogous. Baboon troops are compelled to order themselves in ways which make them effective and coherent as a whole. Artists organize their ideas and materials with the same goal in mind.

Jane Goodall's *In the Shadow of Man* is a fascinating account of animal behavior and social organization in the wild. Goodall studied close-up and in-depth a community of wild chimpanzees in the Gombe Stream area of Tanzania. Her work is considered by many to be a classic of its kind, a shining example of field research with all its frustrations, rigors and rewards. Her field studies involved a community of about forty chimps over a period of ten years. Her observations are detailed, sensitive and all-inclusive, documenting chimpanzee life in total. Throughout her account, one thematic thread consciously and consistently weaves together the varied facets of chimpanzee life. This thread is dominance. Their social structure is based on a dominance hierarchy which involves every male, female and juvenile in the community. Jane Goodall writes, "A chimpanzee community is an extremely complex social organization. The members who compose the community move about in constantly changing associations, and yet, though the society seems to be organized in such a casual manner, each individual knows his place in the social structure—knows his status in relation to any other chimpanzee he may chance upon during the day." She explains that there is an accepted ranking-order among all the members of the chimp community and that this minimizes social friction and competition. Although chimpanzees are very excitable (emotional, if you will), their frequent bursts of rage or anger are ritualized, with roles played according to rank. As a result, rarely do chimps actually hurt each other. It is simply unnecessary. In this case, dominance does not promote violence, it diffuses it.

The dominance hierarchy provides order to the chimpanzee community, all the more precious because the chimps are so excitable. But this order is not the rigid, unyielding order of the military. Rather, it is both flexible and dynamic. Dominance is never decided on one issue, but on a combination of factors—dominance factors. Personality, size, and age are only the more obvious ones. Goodall observed that associations and alliances among individual chimps often became influential in restructuring the accepted ranking-order and sometimes resulted in a new dominant, top-ranking chimpanzee. Similarly, in visual design, a confluence of dominance factors decides the issue of dominance in a pictorial hierarchy which is equally dynamic.

Dominance in Design

Before we begin our discussion of dominance in design, it would be helpful to briefly review our definition of a field-event relationship.

A field consists of a set of characteristics (or properties)—for example, *light, warm* and *transparent*. An event consists of an opposing or differing set of characteristics—for example, *dark, cool* and *opaque.* A field-event relationship, then, consists of two sets of opposing characteristics. If one of these sets gets more attention than the other, it is considered dominant. The dominant set is the event; the subdominant set is the field.

Events are naturally dominant. They tend to stand out in their fields, attract attention and become focal points. In music, the idea of a dominant chord is meaningless without a tonality to base it upon. Like tonality, a field is a "ground" that is built upon or reacted to.

Previously, we postulated a design continuum with a field polarity at one end and an event polarity at the other. The closer a design is to the event polarity, the more it will demonstrate dominance; conversely, the more field-oriented it is, the less it demonstrates dominance. In other words, dominance is intrinsic in all event-oriented design.

To summarize, a field-event relationship is a hierarchical system of organization. It consists of a dominant and a subordinate set of characteristics, providing a natural model for dominance in design.

In a design, there may be one, several, or many field-event relationships. They are divided into three general classes:

1. **Primary Relationships**
2. **Secondary Relationships**
3. **Peripheral Relationships**

Primary Relationships

Primary relationships are central to the conception and form of the design. They impact upon us immediately from a distance or at a glance and are most likely to stay in our memory. Primary relationships are dominant; they always get the most attention. They often involve one or more dominance factors and have a tendency toward high contrast. Their role in the organizational hierarchy is one of leadership.

Secondary Relationships

Secondary relationships are subdominant in the hierarchy of design. They are important without being central. In visual art we don't see them first and in music we don't hear them first, for they tend to be overshadowed by primary relationships. Although they are subordinate, their structural value in design is readily ascertained.

An analogy with chordal harmony in music is helpful in understanding primary and secondary relationships. Aaron Copland explains that "a full chord is always made up of three tones or more, because two-toned chords tend to be ambiguous. A typical full three-toned chord consists of the root (or tonic) and the third and fifth intervals above the root. These would correspond to a field, a secondary event and a primary event in field-event theory. In three-part harmony, the root-third interval may be considered a secondary relationship, the root-fifth a primary relationship. Interestingly, the fifth is also called the "dominant." Most musicians would probably agree that it is a dominance factor in music, both because of its structural value and its ability to attract attention.

Peripheral Relationships

Peripheral relationships are subordinate to both primary and secondary relationships. As the lowest ranking relationships in the design hierarchy, they tend to be subdued and exhibit low contrast. One notices them least, counts them last and forgets them first. They demand little attention, becoming apparent only after close scrutiny. Like peripheral animals in a herd, peripheral relationships are the most expendable; they may be easily shifted, changed or substituted without substantial effect on the main idea of the design or our appreciation of the whole.

Let's use the analogy of three-part harmony once more. Three-tone chords are often made into four-tone chords by simply doubling one of the three tones. This common practice adds weight, depth and color to the chord but has no affect on its structure. This may be considered typical of peripheral relationships and the way they work.

In traditional Western music, and most contemporary music—rock, country-western, and blues—the interval of the "fifth," e.g. G in the key of C, may be considered a "dominance factor" and a "primary relationship."

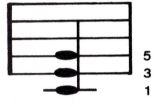

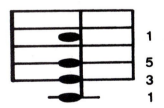

Primary Relationships

Field	Event
Dark	Light
Harmony	Contrast
Negative	Positive
Motion	Position
Simple	Complex
Organic	Geometric
Low-Definition	High-Definition
Subjective	Objective
Informal	Formal
Romantic	Classical

El Greco
Felix Hortensio Paravicino
Oil on canvas. 113 × 86 cm.
Isaac Sweetser Fund
Courtesy, Museum of Fine Arts, Boston

Identify and discuss the "primary relationships" in El Greco's "Felix Hortensio Paravicino."

Primary, Secondary and Peripheral Events

We have just discussed three classes of field-event relationships. This suggests that there are also three classes of events. These are called primary, secondary and peripheral events, and they are also determined by dominance. A primary relationship consists of a primary event and a field, a secondary relationship consists of a secondary event and a field, and so on.

Events tend to dominate each other and establish hierarchies just as relationships do. Although these hierarchies are based on ranking-order, they are neither fixed nor frozen. On the contrary, they are highly dynamic, making design the challenging experience that it is. As artists know, a change in one part of a composition often affects relations in other parts as well, sometimes leading to a total reworking of the idea. Changing a primary event would tend to have that kind of far-reaching impact. However, changing a low-ranking peripheral event would not. The illustration on page 27 shows that the relations between field, primary event, and secondary event are both vital and dynamic.

The terminology and dynamics we have just discussed apply equally well to nonvisual forms of design. For example, music may also be analyzed in terms of primary, secondary and peripheral events. Generally, the subject, or melody, of a piece of music is a primary event in relation to the whole tonal and rhythmic field in which it occurs. But events may also form hierarchies within a specific melodic or rhythmic phrase. In Beethoven's Fifth Symphony, the subject consists of four notes—"de-de-de-da." Although all four notes are clearly essential to the phrase, it is the fourth one—"da"—that gets the most attention: It is a primary event; the "de's" are secondary events. The key point is that a dominance hierarchy is established. In Part III, Dominance Factors, there is a discussion of the various ways in which dominance is established in design, both visual and nonvisual.

Many observers have pointed out that poetry and music are closely related. First of all, they both involve sound. Secondly, they both occur in time—they are temporal designs and therefore rely heavily on meter and rhythm for organization. It follows, then, that we should be able to determine primary, secondary and peripheral events in poetry, much as we do in music. In a verse or line of poetry, certain sounds and words stand out and get more attention; they are primary events, clearly dominant in their fields. For example, in the following line from a poem by T. S. Eliot, we can determine that there is a hierarchy of events and that one of them is dominant:

> In the room the women come and go
> talking of Michelangelo.

The primary event is the word "Michelangelo." It is the word we are most likely to emphasize and remember. The secondary events are "room" and "women"; the remaining words are more or less peripheral events.

In music and poetry, the concept of dominance and a hierarchy of events is as fundamental as it is in visual art; it functions the same way for the same reasons. Finally, the dynamic relations between primary, secondary and peripheral events are essentially similar in all the arts; only the senses being addressed are different. Thus we have an analogical tool that makes it possible to cross academic boundaries in the quest for a comprehensive understanding of design.

In Figure 1, the white area is the event, the black area is the field. In Figure 2, the small black rectangle is the "primary event"; in Figure 3, the white circle is a primary event, the black rectangle a "secondary event." In Figure 4, the small white rectangle is a primary event, the large white rectangle a secondary event. In Figure 5, the black circle is a primary event, the white diamond a secondary event, the white rectangle a "tertiary event." In Figure 6, the white diamond is now a primary event, the black circle a secondary event, the black rectangle tertiary. See if you can determine the "visual logic" behind the shifting classifications of these three events.

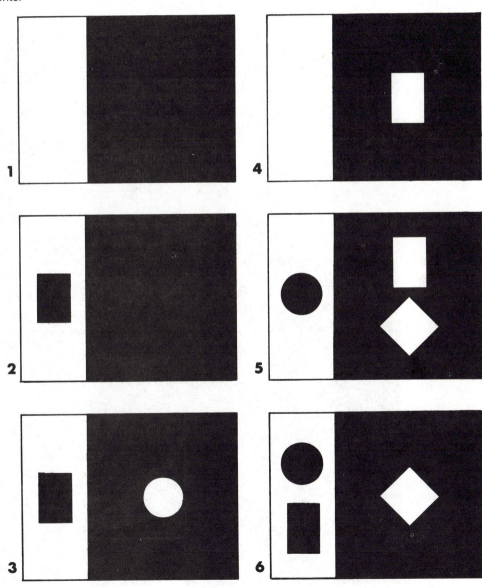

Practicum

The theory of dominance in design is quite sound, for dominance functions in art in the same way that it does in nature. It is a means to an end: order. But, still, it is a theory, and theories have a habit of commanding a great deal of attention for a very short time. How, then, is a theory made to endure? The obvious answer is that it must be useful, practicable and provide a distinct advantage in solving problems.

Field-event theory can readily be made into a working tool by adopting a question and answer format. This should accomplish two basic objectives:

1. **Identify primary relationships**
2. **Identify dominance within these relationships**

Hippolyte Delaroche
Portrait of Marquis de Pastoret
Oil on canvas. 155 × 124.5 cm.
Purchased from the Susan Cornelia Warren Credit Fund
and the Picture Fund
Courtesy, Museum of Fine Arts, Boston

The painting opposite, by Paul Delaroche, is entitled *Portrait of Marquis de Pastoret.* It is a fairly typical nineteenth-century portrait, exceptionally well-designed and painted. Using a question and answer format, let us see if we can come to an understanding of how this remarkable painting was "put together."

Our first task is to identify primary relationships.

Question: What are the primary relationships in this painting?

Answer: light/dark
simple/complex
general/specific
formal/informal
deep/shallow
large/small
geometric/organic

Our second task is to identify dominance within these relationships and, in so doing, determine which characteristic (i.e., light or dark) is "field" and which is "event." This is best accomplished with a series of analytical questions:

Question: Is the painting a *light* field with *dark* in it, or a *dark* field with *light* in it?

Answer: It is a *dark* field with *light* in it.

Question: Which of the two (i.e., light or dark) gets more attention?

Answer: The *light.*

Conclusion: *Light* is the dominant characteristic and constitutes an "event." *Dark* represents the field. Together they constitute a field-event relationship.

Let us try one more.

Question: Is it a *simple* field with *complex* in it, or a *complex* field with *simple* in it?

Answer: A *simple* field with *complex* in it.

Question: Which of the two (i.e., simple or complex) gets more attention?

Answer: The *complex.*

Conclusion: *Complex* is the dominant characteristic and constitutes the event. *Simple* represents the field. Together they form a field-event relationship.

And once again:

Question: Is it a *specific* field with *general* in it, or a *general* field with *specific* in it?

Answer: A *general* field with *specific* in it.

Question: Which of the two gets more attention?

Answer: The *specific*.

Conclusion: *Specific* is the dominant characteristic and constitutes the event. *General* represents the field. Together they form a field-event relationship.

This line of question and answer analysis should continue until all primary relationships have been defined and their dominant characteristics identified. Depending on one's objectives, the analysis can end there or continue with secondary and peripheral relationships until a complete semantic description is achieved.

The question and answer format helps us put theory to work as a problem-solving tool. It is a straightforward, simple procedure, providing a consistent framework in which to think and act. Moreover, it permits the continuous feedback and reinforcement so necessary to the development of self-confidence and self-direction. Each successive group of questions adds to our understanding of relationships and their function in design. In the studio or classroom, the development of critical and problem-solving capabilities is a slow, up-hill struggle, all the more painful when laden with subjective, opinionated dialogue. This question and answer approach, buttressed by a consistent terminology, reduces subjectivity and counters the popular belief that, in art, everything is a matter of personal opinion and taste. It ameliorates the perennial problem of how to discuss art and design objectively and constructively. Finally, it enhances growth and learning by providing a verbal tool for the semantic analysis of design.

The question and answer format works well in the classroom or studio. Critiques proceed smoothly, each answer derived by consensus and discussed. If, however, a question on dominance can't be answered, then we may conclude that dominance is inoperative or has not been established. Consequently, we have no way of distinguishing field from event. There are two probable causes for this:

1. **Unresolved relationships: Dominance has not been determined in the relationship; the design is unresolved.**
2. **Non-hierarchical organization: Dominance is inoperative or intentionally denied; an alternate system of organization (non-hierarchical) is in place.**

Unresolved Relationships

Relationships are articulated by differences. When differences are small or nonexistent, dominance is inoperative; there is no clear ranking-order. This is a quantitative rather than a qualitative problem. For example, if the *amount* of light and dark in a painting is *equal,* we cannot determine dominance. We have no way of knowing whether it is a "light field with dark in it, or a dark field with light in it." The same is true for "warm and cool," "near and far," "simple and complex," "organic and geometric"—the entire inventory of polar adjectives. Old masters and new ones generally avoid equal amounts of opposites (polar adjectives). They eliminate structural ambiguity at the outset, and so should we.

Non-Hierarchical Organization

Non-hierarchical organizations are generally based on uniformity, similarity and harmony. The whole is made up of undifferentiated parts of similar value; all parts are deemed equal. In such systems, there are no outstanding individuals or events. There is no ranking-order and no dominance.

The primary non-hierarchical system of organization is the field. However, fields are not the only non-hierarchical systems to deny dominance; there are several other significant exceptions to the "dominance in design" model:

1. **Symmetry**
2. **Illusions: intentional ambiguity**
3. **Camouflage**
4. **Masking**
5. **Intentional irresolution**
6. **Other rogues, misfits and unforeseens**

Symmetry

If a design is divided in half along a central axis and both halves are identical or similar, it is considered symmetrical. A simple, bisected field shows that dominance is often minimal or absent in symmetry, for both halves are apparently equal. Such designs are ambiguous, displaying a tendency toward the flip-flop, or negative–positive reversal, characteristic of much illusionistic art.

Symmetry is stable and balanced; tension is minimal because energy is in storage. This concept of energy storage is well-illustrated by children on a seesaw: If both children are of **equal** weight, the plank is balanced; it doesn't move. Neither child is dominant. Gravity is momentarily neutralized and the potential energy it implies is in storage. But, should one of the children become bored with this seesaw stand-off and slide off the plank, the other child makes a sudden plunge to the ground—stored energy has been released in full. In either of the two described states, storage—balanced plank—or release—unbalanced plank—there is little or no tension. However, if the children are of **unequal** weights, the plank becomes unstable and unbalanced; the result is tension. Significantly, this tension is highest when children are of **almost** the same weight.

Storage
symmetry

Tension

Dominance

Release
no-tension

In summary:

1. **No difference** . . . . **no dominance** . . . . **no tension**
2. **Small difference** . . . . . **unclear dominance** . . . . **high tension**
3. **Large difference** . . . . . **dominance** . . . . **low tension**

Symmetry may be compared to a balanced plank; energy is in storage, tension is minimal. A condition of no-dominance prevails.

Illusion

What part does dominance play in the creation of illusions? The answer is "no part." In fact, most illusions are based on a calculated denial of dominance. Like paradoxes, they present two sets of conflicting or contradictory signals. These signals are typically of equal strength and compete for the viewer's attention; neither is dominant. The logic of the visual process is temporarily disrupted and the eye becomes overstimulated. As a result, we may see, or think we see, a variety of optical illusions such as vibrations, afterimages, ghost images, flashes, glows or shimmers. However, such illusions are short-lived, for the eye quickly fatigues under this degree of stress and strain. Our cognitive skills are similarly distressed. We may become confused because, without the help of dominance, it is difficult to distinguish between field and event. The usual rational hierarchy becomes defunct; we are faced with an irrational, reversible field-event relationship.

Gestalt psychologists have conducted extensive research on sensory perception and its effects on comprehension. After much experimentation, they concluded that a "correct" reading of figure–ground relationships is an essential first step in visual comprehension. If these relationships are clear and unambiguous, meaning immediately takes shape. We "understand" what we are seeing. However, if they are ambiguous, sensory acuity and comprehension are greatly diminished.

Today, the profile–vase flip-flop illusion is a standard illustration in psychology texts. It is a design calculated to deny figure–ground relationships, making a "correct reading" impossible. We alternately perceive the profiles and the vase as "figure." It is characteristic of such illusions that we cannot see them both at the same time. From this humble beginning, masters of visual literacy like M. C. Escher and Bridget Riley create illusions that deceive the senses and boggle the mind.

Although illusions are meaningful and instructive in their own right, they are doubly valuable for reminding us about the elusive nature of perception. The eye sees, but the brain makes sense of it. Under normal conditions, it is an effortless and automatic process, like breathing. But when faced with ambiguous or paradoxical information, tension and strain immediately ensue and we become suddenly aware of the tenuous relation between our sensory and cognitive processes. "I see," says the viewer, but what he really means is "I *know* what I am seeing." However, in graphic illusions, we see but don't necessarily understand what we see. Our powers of analysis and rational judgment often become useless—true not only of illusions, but of mystical experience in general. "Participation mystique" precludes the most essential element in rational analysis—detachment.

Illusions deny rational relationships by preventing our seeing both field and event at once. Conversely, field-event relationships are designed to guarantee that we *do* see them both at once.

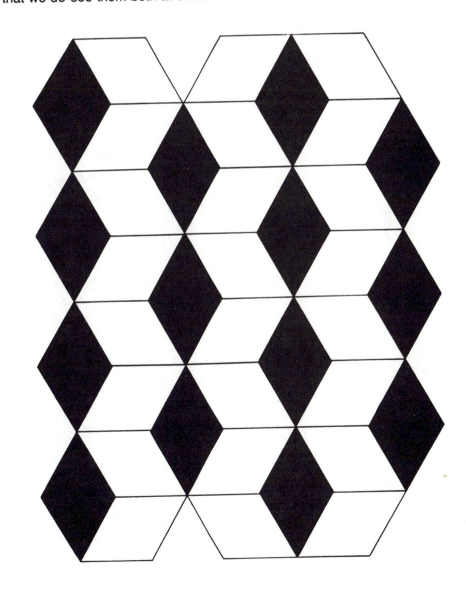

36

M. C. Escher
© Beeldrecht, Amsterdam/V.A.G.A., New York,
Collection Haags Gemeentemuseum,
The Hague, 1981

"Ghost dots," an optical illusion in which gray dots spontaneously appear at the intersections.

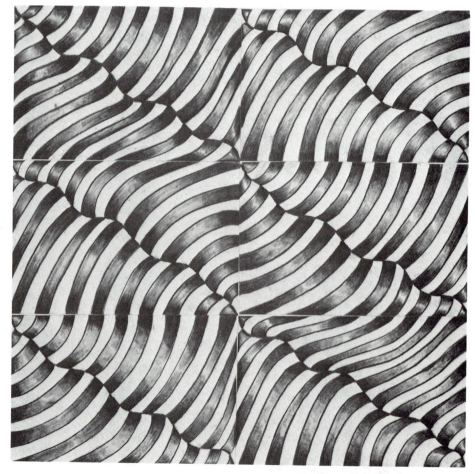

Judith Robbins
Illusion

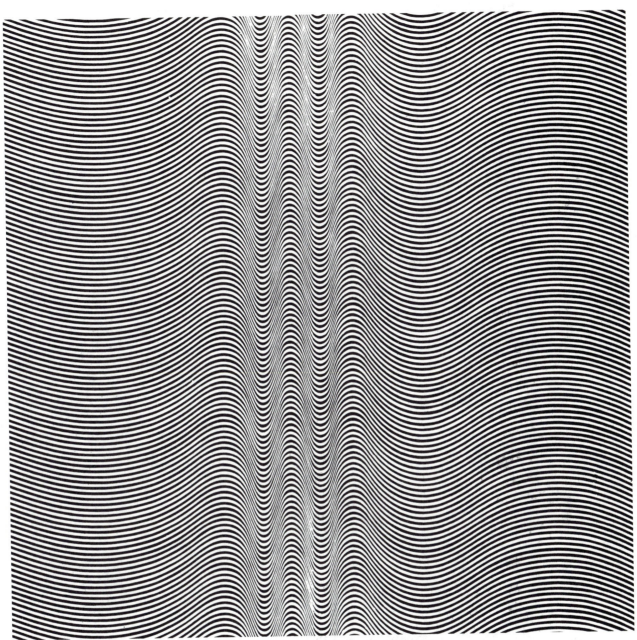

Bridget Riley
Current (1964)
Synthetic polymer paint on composition board
58 3/8 × 58 7/8 in.
Collection, The Museum of Modern Art, New York
Philip Johnson Fund

Illusions have been part of art throughout its history. However, only recently have they been studied separately as an independent form of visual art. Optical art, better known as *op-art*, was probably the first major artistic movement based entirely on optical illusion. Its appeal was predictably high. In a culture in which "seeing is believing," people enjoy a challenge to their senses as well as their intellect. Optical illusions provide a challenge to both.

Depth One of the most familiar visual illusions is that of three-dimensional, pictorial space. We are so accustomed to pictures with depth that we take the illusion quite for granted. However, it is a relatively recent development in pictorial representation, having emerged from the Italian Renaissance only 500 years ago. Since then, an enormous amount of experimentation on ways to articulate space has occurred. Figures 1 through 7 show several common methods for showing depth in design.

1

2

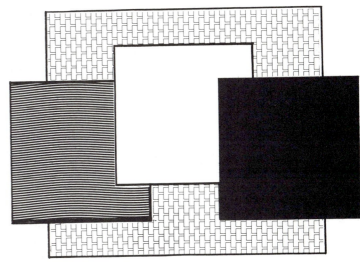

3

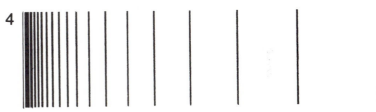

4

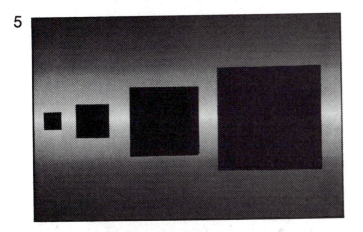

5

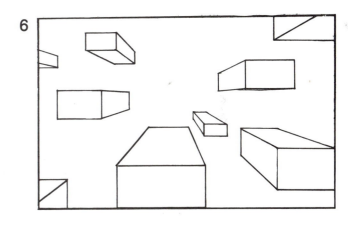

6

7

Seven common ways of creating the illusion of "depth":

1. *Relative size*
2. *Variable density*
3. *Relative position: superimposition, overlap and transparency*
4. *Variable interval*
5. *Sequence and size*
6. *Linear perspective ("convergence")*
7. *Definition ("atmospheric perspective")*

Camouflage

One of the oldest and most familiar visual illusions in nature is animal camouflage. Many animal species employ camouflage as part of their overall survival strategy and would likely perish without it. Woodcock and grouse rely on it for defensive purposes; tiger and cheetah employ it for predatory purposes.

Camouflage is field-oriented. Its purpose is to merge the animal with the environment. It strives for dissolution of form and diminution of contour. It offers concealment rather than revelation. Camouflage is designed to reduce visual acuity by making differentiation difficult. Three factors determine the effectiveness of camouflage:

1. **The distribution of light and dark over the environment**
2. **The distribution of light and dark over the animal**
3. **The degree of similarity of light distribution over the environment and the animal**

If the primary purpose of camouflage is to blend the animal with the environment, then why aren't more animals green like the jungles and forests they inhabit? This sounds at first like an innocently childish question, but it brings us to an interesting point of information—most mammals are color-blind. They see only tonal variation, patterns of light and dark, not color. However, fish and birds do see color and are consequently colorful themselves.

Camouflage is not always simply a matter of blending with the field. There are other ways in which camouflage challenges and subverts vision. For example, some species of animals have decorative coats which do not blend with their environments at all, such as zebras or black and white dairy cattle. Unlike the polar bear, who blends perfectly with his snow-white environment, the zebra stands out in dramatic contrast against his. A zebra is, in fact, a kind of flag. It has the same flamboyant visibility that many flags do—it naturally attracts attention. The question is "Why would a zebra want to attract attention in an environment shared with such dangerous predators as leopards and lions?" To be sure, nature weighs the pros and cons carefully, and so should we. The zebra's chief enemy is the lion, who must single out and separate an individual to make its hunt successful. This is precisely why the zebra's coat is effective. Particularly while the herd is in close formation or moving, individuals mix and merge with each other, creating an ambiguous, dynamic field of black and white stripes. This presents a stiff challenge to the visual sense of the stalking or charging lion and, in the wilderness, a moment's confusion can make the difference between life and death. By merging with each other rather than with the environment, zebras gain an advantage, however minute, which in the long run contributes to the survival of the species.

In the military, both uniforms and equipment are designed to prevent detection by the enemy. Military camouflage reflects the same objectives as animal camouflage. The way in which these objectives are achieved is instructive— by showing us how *not* to be seen, camouflage reveals the underlying principles of visual acuity.

Courtesy of the American Museum of Natural History, New York

Courtesy of the American Museum of Natural History, New York

Masking

In psychology, it is noted that when two sounds are simultaneously proferred, one of them generally becomes harder to hear. This effect is called *masking*. The degree of masking depends on the relationship between the signal (dominant sound) and the masking sound (masker). Maskers are usually subdominant, peripheral or ambient sounds. The relationship between the signal and the masker is determined by three factors:

1. **The intensity of the masker**
2. **The similarity of the masker to the signal**
3. **The field in which the sounds occur**

Intensity refers to the capacity of the masker to affect or mask the signal. A high intensity masker may compete with the signal for dominance in the same way that, in animal societies, a charismatic member may compete with a dominant leader for attention. *Similarity* involves a somewhat different kind of competition—sounds which are similar compete simply because it is difficult to differentiate between them. In other words, as auditory contrast decreases, masking increases. The best way to achieve masking is to surround a sound with a group of similar sounds. Conversely, the best way to distinguish a sound is by surrounding it with a set of opposite or dissimilar sounds. In music, orchestrators and arrangers rely heavily on their knowledge of instrumentation and tone color to put masking into effect. In a sense, it is the imaginative use of masking that gives a piece of music its characteristic form and flavor. Theoretically, a group of uniformly masked sounds can be considered an acoustic field. Masking functions in hearing as camouflage does in seeing; the senses are different, but the principle is the same.

Intentional Irresolution

The main purpose and goal of design is unity, as we have said previously. When unity is attained, a feeling of order and organization is apparent. Forces seem balanced, tensions resolved. The parts relate to the whole in positive fashion—they do not compete. Most works of art and most designs are forged in this context of unity and resolution. When a viewer, or audience, as the case may be, encounters a unified, resolved design in any medium, he or she feels a profound sense of order and is aesthetically moved. He or she enjoys the experience. This is the natural consequence of good design.

But art is diverse. Not all artists pursue the goal of resolution in design; some exploit tension and competition for expressive purposes. In such cases, ir-resolution is intentional—forces remain unstable, tensions unresolved. The artist is willing to risk alienating or irritating his audience—to "leave them hanging,"—in the hope that the message will be more directly perceived and felt. This is more common in temporal media, such as drama, cinema and music, than it is in the plastic arts, but examples may be found in all media. Picasso, Matisse, Leger, Van Gogh, Francis Bacon and Franz Kline are a few of the artists who have, on occasion, employed intentional irresolution in painting.

In Western music, the concept of tension and release (resolution) has deep and broad roots. It pervades most of our music. We are conditioned to expect that all melodic phrases and chord progressions will move inevitably toward resolution, sometimes called *consonance.* But the dictum of consonance was challenged early in the twentieth century by composers such as Debussy, Stravinsky and Schoenberg. In fact, Schoenberg abandoned the principle of tonality completely, pursuing instead a new-sounding music based on dis-sonance.

Dissonance is calculated irresolution; sounds are permitted to compete or clash. Of course, such music tends to be tension-filled and is not easy to listen to, but its expressive potential is indisputable. In more recent times, John Cage challenged not only tonality and consonance but the entire con-cept of aesthetics in musical design. Although an accomplished pianist him-self, he chose to experiment with unorthodox "sound-sources"—radios, kitchen appliances, tape recorders. Obviously, a John Cage concert rarely resulted in a feeling of order and resolution for the audience.

In the early 1960s, New Wave Jazz emerged as a violently dissonant, rev-olutionary musical form, led by composer-musicians like Charles Mingus and Albert Ayler. Their aim was to express the bitterness and frustration of the black man in contemporary urban society. To achieve this, the traditional concepts of melody, harmony, tonality and resolution were all temporarily rejected. Tension was purposely heightened and left unresolved, expressing the very condition which gave it birth.

In summary, artists sometimes find it necessary to abandon traditional notions of design in order to express their unique feelings and ideas. Understandably, such excursions into unmapped artistic terrain tend to be highly charged with emotion and filled with risk. Vigorous but exhausting, they are usually short-lived. But intentional irresolution remains a viable option; it will always be part of the spectrum of activities we call art.

Principle of Unequal Division

Tomisawa Hanzaburo
Scene of Two Actors
Woodblock print
Courtesy, Museum of Fine Arts, Boston

As most artists know by experience, changing the amount of some characteristic, such as light, often leads to the solution of a problem. "I think it needs a little more, ahh . . ." the painter is heard to say. In design, quality is routinely influenced by judgments about quantity. All phenomena that involve quantity (number, frequency or amount) have a proclivity toward pattern, and from pattern, a principle may sometimes be gingerly coaxed.

The Principle of Unequal Division

The principle of unequal division is a working tool, an instrument for problem-solving in design. Its premise is deceptively simple: Relationships consisting of equal amounts of opposites preclude dominance and tend to generate structural ambiguity and a state of irresolution. The *principle of unequal division* states: ***Avoid equal amounts of opposites in design.*** This is a general principle, helpful in design decision-making in any and all media. It can be expanded, with some loss of conciseness, to: Avoid equal or ***almost*** equal amounts of opposites in all but symmetrical designs, illusions and fields.

Relationships in which elements are ***almost equal*** are particularly tense and tenuous. They often exhibit a competitiveness that is unhealthy and stressful in both pictorial and social systems. Celebrated natural scientist Konrad Lorenz explains: "All social animals are status-seekers, hence there is always particularly high tension between individuals who hold *immediately adjoining positions* in the ranking order. Conversely, this tension diminishes the further apart the two animals are in rank." Similarly in design, there is more innate tension between a circle and an oval than a circle and a square. It is over small differences in attention-getting power (dominance) that colors, shapes, sizes or spaces clash. Lorenz identified a principle in nature, based on his observations of jackdaws, greylag geese and coral fish, which applies equally well to visual design.

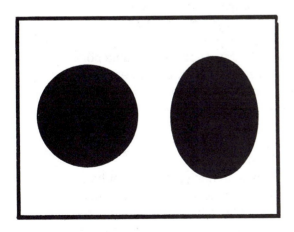 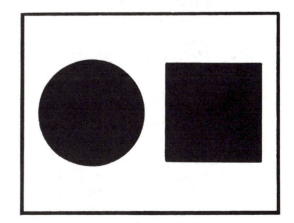

48

We have made an analogy between individual animals in a hierarchy and shapes in a design, exploring the principle that tension is generated by small differences. But shapes are visual elements; what of our other senses? Do they also follow this principle?

With the help of a synthesizer, it is possible to show that Lorenz's principle also applies to our auditory sense. If two oscillators are tuned to the same frequency, they reinforce each other, sounding louder. But if we change the frequency of one just *slightly,* the result is instant, irritating dissonance. Although there is only a small difference between the two frequencies, great tension is generated as they compete for dominance. Furthermore, as the difference between them increases, tension decreases. There is an apparent parallel between individuals competing for dominance in a group, shapes competing for attention in design, and sounds competing in music.

In our discussion of symmetry, a seesaw is used to illustrate the same point about tension and dominance. Briefly, it is noted that two children of the same weight balance each other; there is neither tension nor dominance. But if one weighs *slightly* less, tension develops as the plank seesaws tentatively between them. As you have probably guessed by now, tension decreases as the difference in weight increases.

In summary, the principle of unequal division is an analytical tool that helps us to avoid ambiguity and tension in design. It specifically identifies small differences as a major cause of tension, particularly in its effect on sensory perception. Finally, its application to other disciplines in the arts and sciences is yet to be explored.

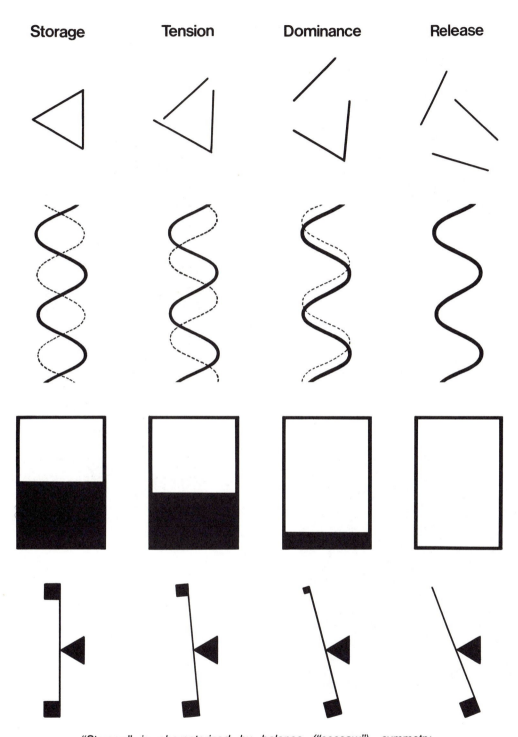

| Storage | Tension | Dominance | Release |

"Storage" is characterized by balance ("seesaw"), symmetry (bisected rectangle), cancellation (opposing wave-forms) and closure (equilateral triangle). "Tension" is characterized by small differences in weight, size, wave-phase or alignment; "dominance" by large differences. "Release" is characterized by the absence of opposing force: one-sided seesaw, solid rectangle (unified field), in-phase waves (reinforcement) and three random lines (dispersion).

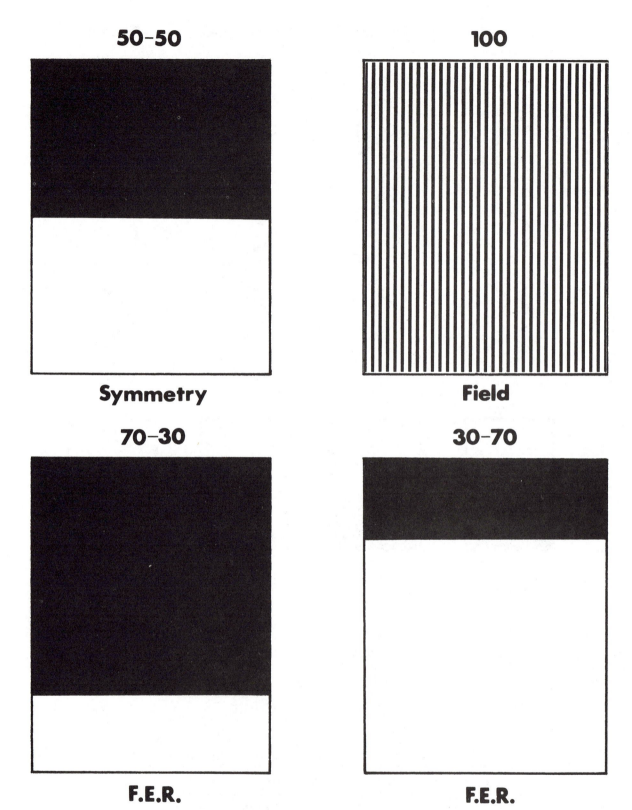

50-50

Symmetry

100

Field

70-30

F.E.R.

30-70

F.E.R.

Relationships based on 70%–30% ratios display apparent dominance and have least ambiguity and tension. They are generally the most stable field-event relationships (F.E.R.).

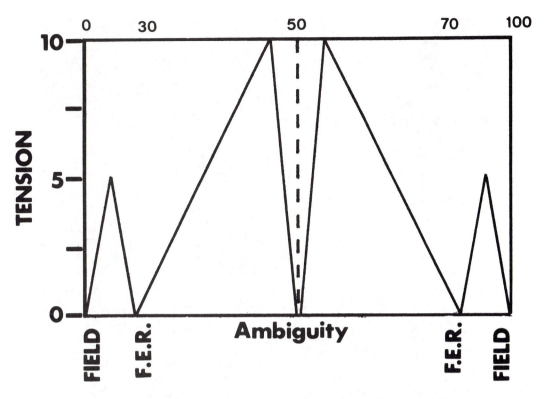

The diagram above shows that tension reaches a peak (10) just before and after the halfway mark (50); so does ambiguity. Tension is minimal at 30 and 70, but rises again at the extremes—just after 0 and before 100. Field-event relationships with 30–70 ratios have minimal tension and maximum stability.

DOMINANCE

FIELD-EVENT RELATIONSHIP

NO TENSION

Perception and Dominance

Sensory perception is surprisingly consistent and uniform considering the immense complexity of many of our sensory mechanisms. By and large, people all over the world process sensory data in essentially the same way; we share a common physiology. But most people are not consciously aware of the actual means by which they see, hear, touch, taste, and smell. These processes are largely involuntary and function beneath the threshold of ordinary human awareness; they work without our giving them a thought. However, there are patterns and systems that help our sensorium to function; among the most important of these is dominance.

Dominance is essential in sensory perception. It is a central link in a chain of psycho-physiological processes that includes sensation, differentiation and identification. Sensory information, like all information, must be differentiated to be meaningful; contrast is the vehicle that makes this possible. Indeed, without contrast our senses would be quite useless. But it is dominance that does the final work of clarifying meaning and ascertaining relative value. Without it, there is little hope of organizing the constant stream of sensory information with which we must daily cope. We would be cast adrift on a sea of sensation without a compass, map, guide or pilot. In essence, differentiation, contrast and dominance are the navigational instruments of the sensorium. Dominance is built into the system. Whether it is expressed as preference, mechanics or biologic imperative, it always serves one master—organization. When dominance is at work, visual comprehension is spontaneous and sensory acuity is at its best; but when it is not, sensory acuity rapidly declines. Acoustic masking, discussed previously, is a perfect illustration of this. Without the help of dominance, our senses cannot fulfill their mission of differentiation. Sensory data degenerates into obscurity, confusion and ambiguity. It is, however, precisely this ambiguity which provides the key to optical illusions, which generally spring from a condition of no-dominance. In art, this may be purposeful and part of the artist's personal aesthetic sensibility, but in most other contexts, it wreaks havoc on our senses.

In sensory perception, the psychological mood created by conditions of no-dominance is one of anxiety and tension. Our senses are alternately confounded, dulled and irritated. The longer dominance desists, the more redundant our emotions become; we get bored or annoyed. Understandably, our subjective response is "I don't like it." In sensory perception, conditions of no-dominance generally result in:

1. **ambiguity and confusion**
2. **undifferentiated generalization (i.e., sensory scanning)**
3. **tension and anxiety**
4. **reduced sensory acuity**
5. **overstimulation (optical illusions, afterimages and color vibrations)**
6. **sensory fatigue**
7. **irritation and discomfort (see "critical fusion")**
8. **passivity and dejection**

It is a natural human tendency to eliminate ambiguity and resolve tension whenever possible. This is more than a mechanical reaction; it is a perceptual and conceptual imperative. The terms *leveling* and *sharpening* describe typical human responses to ambiguity—we try to eliminate differences (leveling) or increase them (sharpening). Gestalt psychologists found that we spontaneously correct small differences in shapes or figures that we see to reduce ambiguity and tension. Their conclusions, derived by experiment under controlled conditions, dovetail nicely with those of the naturalist, Konrad Lorenz, made in the wild.

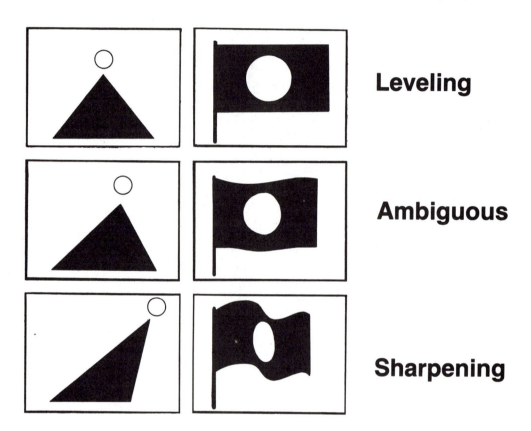

Leveling

Ambiguous

Sharpening

Leveling, Sharpening, and Creativity

On a more conceptual plane, the process of leveling and sharpening may shed some light on the nature of creativity and on art itself. In general, people seem to have a built-in bias towards leveling; it is easier to recount stock, conventional models than to forge new ones. Their natural tendency is toward conservatism, holding to a so-called norm. There are distinct advantages to this bias—it reinforces community behavioral patterns while minimizing stress and strain on both individuals and societies. Indeed, nature would concur with this strategy. However, leveling also has some disadvantages—it tends to inhibit change, chance and creativity. For this reason, artists have a bias

Identify and discuss examples of "leveling" and "sharpening" above. Make a sequence of designs which illustrates the process of leveling and sharpening.

of their own—towards sharpening. The artist sees differently, we say, but that doesn't really explain very much. How and why does he see differently? The artist's vision is often shaped by a process of conceptual sharpening in which differences are starting points for exploration and discovery. This process, identical in all the arts and sciences, encourages analogy, metaphor and hypothesis. It invites inquiry and experimentation. Much of the abstraction and figurative distortion in modern art arises from this process of conceptual sharpening. In this context, leveling and sharpening are antithetical—one promotes convention, the other, invention. Art is a counterpoint to the pervasive leveling tendency of modern society.

DOMINANCE
FACTORS

PART
III

Paul Gauguin
D'où Venons Nous? Que Sommes Nous? Où Allons Nous?
Oil on canvas. 139 × 374.5 cm.
Arthur Gordon Tompkins Residuary Fund
Courtesy, Museum of Fine Arts, Boston

How is Dominance Established?

As one might well imagine, there are many ways to establish dominance in a design. To explore them all would be both an unnecessary and impossible task; however, we can identify several outstanding characteristics, attributes and behaviors that commonly contribute to dominance. These are called *dominance factors.* The following is an inventory of twenty major dominance factors.

Dominance Factors

Light
Contrast
Definition
Presence
Condition
Number
Size
Position
Color
Temperature
Motion
Orientation
Direction
Shape
Configuration
Texture
Dissimilarity
Frequency
Cathexis
Content

Philip Paratore
Earthrise (detail)
Oil on panel

Light

Light from the sun warms, energizes and illuminates the earth. It is unquestionably the dominant factor in visual perception, for without light, there is no sight. Phototropism is essential in plants: they faithfully follow the light that nourishes them. But it is operative in animals and humans as well. In a darkened room we automatically turn toward a bright window, a candle or a television set. In the theater, lighting is of the utmost importance in achieving dramatic impact. Centuries ago Rembrandt revealed the expressive power of light with a mastery that has rarely been equalled. Candelabras, campfires and the bright lights of Broadway are familiar symbols of light and its hypnotic effect on people. "To see the light" is to be enlightened. Our smartest people are called "brilliant." In summary, light is one of the major dominance factors in design.

Vision

In the course of a day, the amount of light approaching the eye is always changing, depending on the situation and the source. Light comes to us in an extremely broad range of intensities. How does the eye accommodate such widely varied levels of light and maintain the constancy and normalcy we take for granted? The eye responds to changing intensities of light by either closing or opening the iris, like a lens diaphragm in a typical 35-mm camera. Both the eye and the camera are designed to maintain constancy by adjusting the size of the opening through which light enters. Whenever we look at an intense light source such as an electric lamp or sunlit window, our irises automatically contract. Sunlight reflecting off snow or water as glare makes us squint, bringing the eyelid and lash into play. A sudden flash of brilliant light causes blinking, to the dismay of many a flashbulb photographer. In the eye, constant illumination may not always be achieved, but it is always the goal.

However, the physiology of the eye, with its adjustable lens and iris, is not perfect. The iris opens when the light level is low, closes when it is high. Thus, the amount of entering light is theoretically kept constant. But, when the iris closes to reduce the intensity of light, it simultaneously causes a darkening of the darks and shadow areas. This is most evident when an intense light source is located behind an object (backlit)—the object tends to blacken out, as well as flatten out. Objects or figures placed in front of a window (silhouetted) are equally hazardous. As most photographers quickly learn, this results in a loss of detail and definition in the shadow areas which have become inadvertently darkened. In the process of maintaining constancy of light, the dark range has been both shortened and deepened. This seems to suggest a bias toward high-contrast imagery, dominated by normally bright lights and extra-deep darks. Aura and halo effects are familiar dramatizations of this bias and have been used effectively by artists, from Leonardo da Vinci to Walt Disney.

The interface between light and dark reveals much—both are intensified at the edge. This sometimes results in a subtle glow, especially where the edge is crisp and sharp. The same pattern of overstimulation and fatigue that causes afterimages also causes glowing effects. Staring at the edge accelerates eye fatigue and will usually enhance the glow. One of the practical effects of this glow is to demarcate edges clearly. Complementary colors are similarly intensified at the edge but don't merely glow—they vibrate. In color vibrations, definition may be decreased rather than increased, because the edge appears to be moving.

Brightness is normally perceived and measured in relation to a field or background. A bright figure looks brighter on a dark field, and conversely, a dark figure looks darker on a bright field. Perceptual illusions of this kind are so commonplace that their significance is likely to be overlooked. They are keys to visual acuity.

The illusion of increasing brightness in the white circle is caused by the increasing darkness of the surrounding field—evidence of the relative nature of light–dark perception.

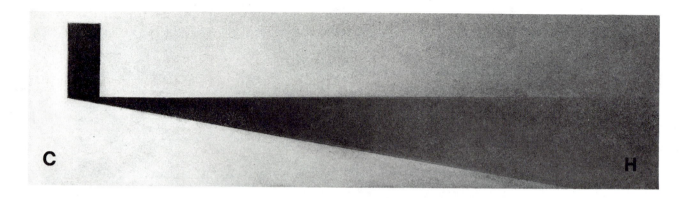

A shadow cast by a simple object shows us that the brightest light and the darkest dark occur simultaneously at the point closest to the light source. The shadow edge is highly defined at that point but gradually becomes diffused as the distance from the light source increases. Beginning in high-contrast at point (C), both light and shadow concurrently grade toward gray, eventually blending in edgeless harmony at point (H). The cast shadow provides us with a compact and elegant model of the harmony-contrast continuum.

An intensely bright light requires an equally intense dark—its precise complement. Should the required dark not be present, a state of tension exists. The eye and brain work to resolve this tension by supplying the missing complement. They usually do this by shifting away from the light and toward the dark, that is, away from the dominant and toward the subdominant. The goal is polar resolution.

The eye has engaged a strategy of polarity in its timeworn parlance with the rich, ever-changing world of light and dark. But all poles have a middle-ground—an "equator." In vision, this is called a "constant," and is part of a larger human tendency toward moderation and conservatism. This tendency has obvious survival value for both sensoriums and societies: it minimizes stress and shock, maximizes stability. Moreover, it enhances balance by providing a relative center. The dynamic interplay between center and poles is ceaseless and filled with lessons, for it is one of the great recurrent themes of nature.

"Seeing" is deceptively simple. Trying to understand it can be a challenging, sometimes bewildering experience. On the other hand, it can also be exhilarating, even mystical. For example, in the convoluted logic of vision, the sensation of light is often increased by adding dark, and vice versa. This is like saying we lose weight by eating more! But drop a single spot of black on a white page; the white *will* look brighter around the spot. This sounds more like magic than logic, but is nevertheless an accurate account. Vibrations, halos, auras, "ghost" images, afterimages and optical illusions in general are all close cousins of magic: they occur in the eye of the beholder and cannot be objectively attributed to reality.

Light

Light and dark as flat pattern.

Light and the illusion of spatial depth.

Michael Lewis
Untitled
Oil on paper

And Dark

Rembrandt van Rijn
Rembrandt's Father
Oil on canvas. 75 × 60 cm.
Purchased from Arthur Rotch Fund
Courtesy, Museum of Fine Arts, Boston

Rembrandt van Rijn
Doctor Faustus
Etching on oatmeal paper
Gift of Miss Ellen Bullard
Courtesy, Museum of Fine Arts, Boston

A Summary

1. The polar relation between light and dark is essential to vision.

2. The light–dark polarity is analogous in vision and design.

3. A relative center or "constant" is implicit in the light–dark polarity.

4. When a light and dark of equal intensity are juxtaposed, they are perceived as complete and whole. This may be called polar resolution.

5. Light and dark are relative; either may be shifted by the eye to achieve:
   a. constancy
   b. polar resolution.

6. Polarity is expressed by contrast; it intensifies sensation, heightens luminosity and increases visual acuity.

7. The interface between light and dark is dynamic; action is intensified at the edge.

8. Optical illusions are based on two competing signals; neither is dominant.

9. Light is a dominance factor. It naturally attracts attention.

10. Differentiation, contrast and dominance function similarly in vision and design.

Contrast

Contrast is the key differentiating agent in both sensory perception and design. It articulates and defines differences. Without contrast, differences fade
and, consequently, so does dominance. On the other hand, contrast sharpens
definition and heightens sensation. A police siren in the still of night, a pair
of crows in a snow-white field and a bold line drawn through fuzzy tones all
illustrate the expressive power of contrast. Our eyes are naturally attracted
by contrast, just as they are by light. It is a major factor in design and
perception.

Contrast

Contrast may be generally defined as differentiation, for wherever there are differences, there is contrast. Sometimes the differences are large, as in white versus black; sometimes they are small, as in gray versus black; and sometimes they are negligible, as in cool black versus warm black. Large differences denote high contrast, small differences denote low contrast, and negligible differences show no contrast.

Contrast is characterized by a general tendency to stand apart or stand out, that is, to be "outstanding." Individual elements assert their identity. Contrast is a unifying force—it creates wholes by the juxtaposition of differences. This is called *polar resolution.*

The key differentiating agent in all relationships is contrast; without it, field-event relationships can be neither articulated nor perceived. Precise opposites yield maximum contrast and maximum differentiation. They produce field-event relationships that are dramatically graphic and have great attention-getting power. This is demonstrated by color complements which sit precisely opposite each other in a relationship of polarity. Red and green are typical; their effect on each other is mutual excitement and intensification. The beholder's eye is dazzled by the intensity of the contrasting color sensation. This familiar phenomenon leads us to a central point: Sensory perception is universally heightened by contrast.

The relationship between light and dark reveals a polar juxtaposition of great utility and eloquence, one that has engaged philosophers, poets, scientists, and artists for as long as people have been conscious of themselves and their world.

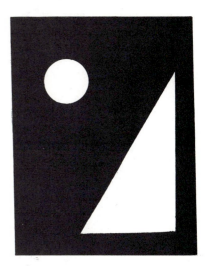

In traditional Oriental philosophy, differences were cohered into wholes by means of contrast. There was little distinction between philosophy, poetry and reality in the "old China," for all were perceived and articulated in terms of opposition according to the all-encompassing system of Yin and Yang. This system springs from one deceptively simple perception: Opposites form complete wholes when joined together. In this image of the world, there is no day without night, life without death or form without space. The delicacy of this intuition cannot easily be appreciated by the rational and materialistic sensibility of the modern, literate Westerner. The Yin–Yang symbol vividly illustrates this conception of union and the primeval graphic power of contrast.

Contrast

Light	Dark
Simple	Complex
Geometric	Organic
Large	Small
Angular	Circular
Shallow	Deep
Defined	Undefined
Classical	Romantic

Philip Paratore
Tales of Old Amsterdam
Oil on canvas. 40 × 40 in.

*Identify and discuss eight dif-
ferent forms of contrast in
"Tales of Old Amsterdam."*

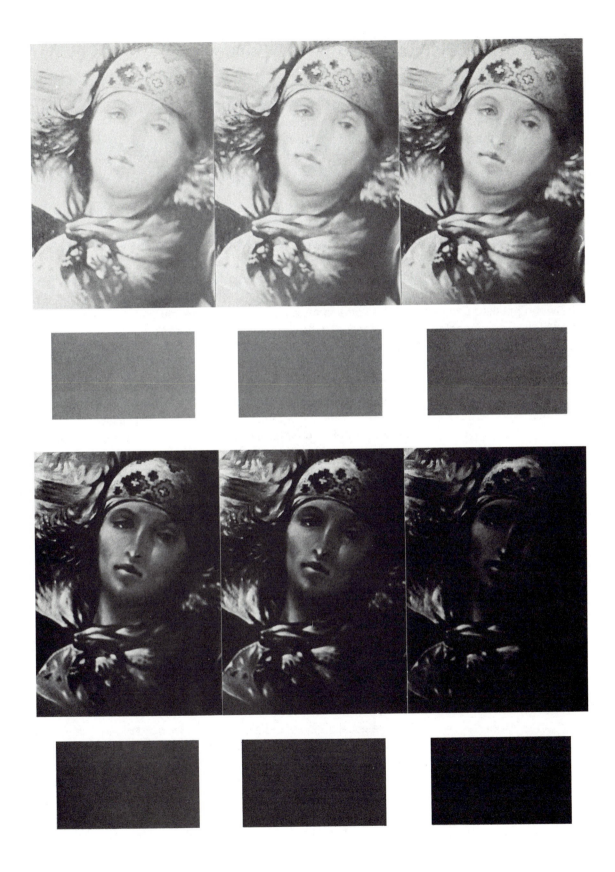

Disorganized acoustic fields are experienced as noise, typified by a badly tuned radio station, an untuned guitar or a mix of overlapping conversations at a party. Static and hum are often highly organized fields, although considered noise because they are devoid of content. Synthesizers are circuited to produce noise systematically by mixing frequencies—white noise contains all frequencies and sounds something like "shhuuush. . . ." Add echo/reverb, run it through the envelope-shaper to suggest rising and falling, and the result sounds like wind and surf at the seashore. White light, like white noise, contains all frequencies.

Like visual stimuli, acoustic stimuli are perceived and differentiated in terms of relationships. Auditory contrast is as vital to hearing as visual contrast is to seeing. Both musical and ambient sounds are perceived in relative degrees of contrast to their acoustic fields. When masking is high, contrast is insufficient and auditory acuity decreases. Music sounds unclear; it becomes blurred and blended in a kind of acoustic stew. Any change in the relationships between masked and unmasked sounds in music engenders a new perception and a corresponding change of mood. In turn, our changing mood greatly affects the music and the listening experience itself.

Chants, chorales and drones are musical forms associated with harmony. They tend to create simple fields, often consisting of massed, unison voices. Unison is itself an organizational idea that expresses oneness and togetherness. Tibetan chants, Indian ragas and European chorales are field-oriented musical forms and contain little acoustic contrast. Generally speaking, religious music tends toward harmony rather than contrast; it generates moods of group unity descendant from our deepest tribal past. On the other hand, the vast majority of worldly, Western music is contrast-oriented. Music based on auditory contrast is easily discerned; it always features a soloist. Whether a virtuoso pianist in a Beethoven symphony, the first violin in a Bartok concerto or the lead guitar in a B. B. King blues number, the soloist is the focal point of our listening attention. Elvis Presley was widely considered "the King of Rock and Roll" and, like all first-rate monarchs, was the ultimate soloist. The Beatles may not have dethroned Presley, but they certainly "shook-up" his monarchy by expressing the new tribal, collective consciousness of Electric Age youth.

The very concept of a soloist presumes a hierarchical structure with the same dynamics of dominance we have seen elsewhere.

The classical music of India is characterized by harmony in the general sense of the word. Like most tribal or religious music, it is essentially field-oriented. The basic musical form is the raga. It stresses overall, organic pattern rather than melody or motif, and lacks the dominant solo voice to which we are accustomed in Western music. The raga also emphasizes emotional development; it has a meditative quality, encouraging spiritual feelings and an attitude of repose in both performers and audience.

Harmony

Harmony is an expression of order in art: to harmonize is to organize. History shows that it is a pervasive concept, touching all periods, styles and mediums. The classical sculpture of ancient Greece, the luminous landscapes of French Impressionists and the austere canvases of contemporary American field painters are all familiar expressions of harmony in art.

Harmony

Harmony is defined in Webster's New Collegiate Dictionary as "agreement between parts of a design or composition giving unity of effect or an aesthetically pleasing whole." It is further defined as "concord in facts, opinions, interests, etc." Harmony is characterized by likenesses, uniformity and a general tendency to merge and blend. Individual elements do not stand out; they relinquish their identity to the whole. Harmony is a unifying force.

Tribal Harmony

Anthropologists have long understood the importance of harmony as a primary principle of social organization among tribal cultures. The emphasis in such cultures is always on the clan or the tribe as a whole. Individual identity is markedly less important, a fact attested to by vast bodies of anonymous art characteristic of tribal cultures throughout the world. Anthropologist Edmund Carpenter writes, "Tribal men everywhere regard themselves as integral parts of nature." Harmony is inherent in their perception of themselves and their world.

In traditional Oriental philosophy, harmony has exalted spiritual value, symbolizing both freedom and ultimate fulfillment. The great Taoist and Buddhist teachers of the Far East called for the merging of oneself with nature and the infinite cosmos in a kind of transcendental union. This union with the universe implies a loss of self and, like all unions, is antithetic to individualism in general. Transcendence through harmony is a common theme throughout the religions of the Far East.

Musical Harmony

In music, harmony is a technique for organizing groups of different but related tones. These tones are called consonant and, when sounded together, form chords, Although chords are made of separate tones or voices, harmony ensures that they sound as one and are "in concert." Whether we are listening to the Beatles, a barbershop quartet, or the local church choir, the blend of voices in harmony always conveys a feeling of agreement and kinship among the members of the group.

About a thousand years ago, anonymous medieval composers began experimenting with crude forms of harmony, the earliest of which was called *organum.* In organum, the melody was simultaneously voiced at intervals of a fourth below and a fifth above the tonic, creating a simple, rather austere harmony. Because the melody was identical or parallel in all three voices, it was apparently first conceived as a variation of unison. Be that as it may, the importance of organum as a musical innovation can hardly be overestimated, for it opened the door to ten centuries of involvement with the concept of melodic harmony in Western music.

Fields are organized on the basis of harmony. Differentiation and contrast are minimal but that is not to say that contrast is precluded. Should contrast occur as a "uniform characteristic in time and space," the result is a field. A black and white checkerboard is a familiar example of a field created by a uniform distribution of contrast. On the other hand, a blank white page is a field with no contrast. Both the checkerboard and the blank page conform equally well to the definition of a field; harmony is the key unifying agent in fields.

Unified fields, whether organic or geometric, are characterized by consistency and "harmony."

Harmony-Contrast Continuum

Field-event theory postulates a continuum in which fields and field-event relationships are the poles. They are shaped in two basic ways:

1. **Harmony**
2. **Contrast**

Harmony and contrast represent polarities, functioning as two ends of a continuum. Between the harmony pole and the contrast pole are as many steps as one wishes to contemplate, each occupying a unique position on the continuum. Just as we grade a series of steps from light to dark to produce a visual gray scale, we may similarly construct a graded scale for harmony and contrast.

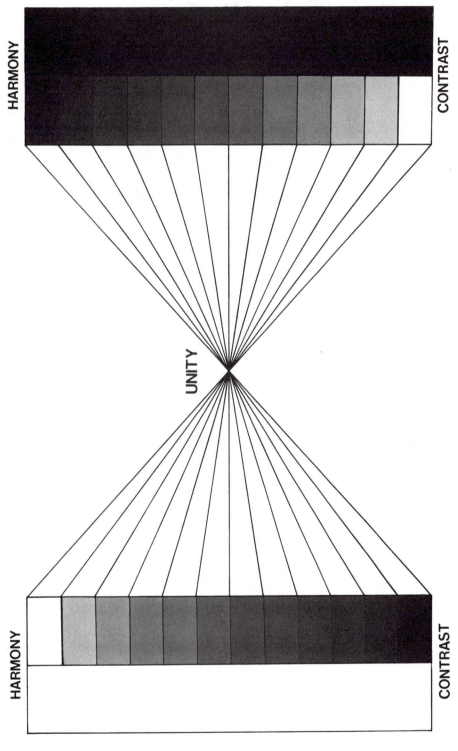

This "continuum" diagram shows that harmony and contrast are part of a continuum: as harmony increases, contrast decreases and vice versa. It also shows that harmony and contrast both lead to unity, the general goal of good design.

Harmony-Contrast Continuum

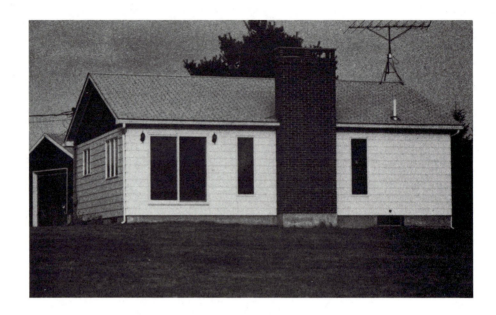

Definition

Information that is clear, complete and well-defined is said to have "high-definition." It is easy to see, understand and remember. Still photographs tend to be high in definition, as do architects' drawings, instruction manuals and documentary movies. In acoustics and sound reproduction, this is called high fidelity, or *hi-fi.* Accuracy and precision are at a premium; distortion is systematically eliminated. In visual design, high-definition elements are characterized by high-contrast, exact lines, sharp edges, clarity and completeness. The eye is naturally attracted to such highly defined elements; consequently, they tend to be dominant.

Human vision is characterized by two basic muscular behaviors: focusing and scanning. High-definition information encourages focusing; low-definition information invites scanning. Moreover, by focusing our eyes, we focus our attention, suggesting an analogy between vision and consciousness itself.

Focusing   **Scanning**

High-definition, high-contrast information maximizes sensory acuity—stimulation is apparently high. Everything is in focus—little is left to the imagination. There is no uncertainty and therefore little or no tension. Rather, a feeling of resolution ensues. On the other hand, low-definition, low-contrast information is more apt to generate tension and anxiety because it is not clear and focused. We must work much harder to "get the message." It requires more effort, more involvement and, quite often, more risk. Consequently, it carries a potentially higher emotional charge.

High-definition design stresses position over movement—everything has a correct place within an orderly, stable structure. We can return to the same point, word, phrase, note, beat, mark, shape, figure, element or event over and over again because its position is clearly stated and unchanging. In design, as in nature, position and movement are polarities—as the value of position increases, that of motion or movement decreases. This suggests that Robert Ardrey's "territorial imperative" applies only to highly defined, positional animal societies. Furthermore, there is a tempered linkage between high-definition, position, rank-order, hierarchy and dominance.

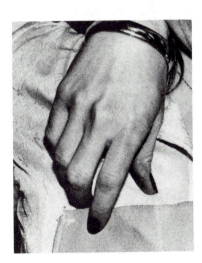

High-Definition

The relationship between high- and low-definition events is of key importance in visual design. As we have discussed previously, high-definition events encourage focusing, both our eyes and our attention. This is especially true when high-definition is coupled with high-contrast. Such events are like visual anchors—our eyes move from these highly defined, dominant events outward toward less defined events; scanning gradually replaces focusing. The result is a natural, perception-oriented system of organization that encompasses the entire visual field.

Albrecht Durer
Melancholia I
Engraving. 14 × 18 in.
Gift of Miss Ellen T. Bullard
Courtesy, Museum of Fine Arts, Boston

Low-Definition

Philip Paratore
Birth Song
Oil on panel
48 × 60 in.

Definition and Language

BABY, PLEASE DON'T GO
BABY, PLEASE DON'T GO
—
BABY, PLEASE DON'T GO
BACK TO NEW ORLEANS
—
YA KNOW I LOVE YA SO
BABY, PLEASE DON'T GO
—

Doctors and lawyers choose their words carefully. They place great value on clarity and comprehension of meaning in speech, for misunderstanding could easily lead to disaster—the loss of a client or a patient. In their practices, words must be precise. They must say exactly what needs to be said without unnecessary embellishment; they leave no room for interpretation or error. The language of doctors and lawyers is highly defined. It is formal, positional and domineering, similar to high-definition graphics in visual design. On the other hand, *jargon* and *slang* are modes of language that place little value on word meaning or content. The emphasis is on the more evocative, expressive qualities of speech: sound, texture, intonation and rhythm. Understandably, youths often shun high-definition language as a symbol of adult or institutional authoritarianism. Social minorities develop their own slang-filled dialects for essentially the same reason. The music of youth or minority subcultures illustrates the same point—form is stressed over content; consequently, language incorporated as lyrics is low in definition. In singing the blues, it is not word meaning that counts but feeling. Lawyers and blues singers are on opposite ends of the language spectrum. In music, definition is an index to form, style, audience and social milieu.

Generally speaking, poetry is a "bluesy" idiom. It relies heavily on the evocative power of language as sound: tone, timbre, texture, rhythm, contour and so on. Like all mediums that condense or compress information, poetry, whether it is written or spoken, tends to be low in definition. It is suggestive rather than explanatory. It invites the audience into the domain of metaphor and imagination. At its best, poetry evokes profound ideas and feelings with few words. Japanese haiku expresses well this concept of poetry.

The snow melts:
Bamboos uncoil themselves
Where the sunlight falls.

> Masaoka Shiki
> *Modern Japanese Haiku*
> *An Anthology*

"Winter Fête"
The cascade resounds behind operetta huts.
Fireworks prolong,
through the orchards and avenues near the Meander,
—the greens and reds of the setting sun.
Horace nymphs with First Empire headdresses.
—Siberian rounds and Boucher's Chinese ladies.

> Arthur Rimbaud

A Report on the Weather Here

Wolf weather
wind-rake and moonblister
it chills and hare
to his hole
and will enter into a man
bent low
to the guttering smokedrift of campfires.

Somehow we fit in,
fleshed gear-teeth to the sprocket
and are turned.

> Terry Plunkett

Highly defined events or elements have presence. They appear to be closer, clearer, sharper and brighter. As a result, it is possible to give information about location in space (spatial depth) by the way we define edges and forms. If high-definition indicates presence, then low-definition indicates distance. In this visual dialogue of "close" and "far," we have a simple system for the articulation of spatial depth.

In photography, depth-of-field refers to the amount of imagery in focus at one time. While beginners may have a natural prejudice toward clear pictures, an experienced photographer often uses sharp focus selectively, for spatial organization or other aesthetic reasons. In this context, it is not unusual to leave the foreground out of focus in order to direct attention to something in the middleground, a technique also used in cinematography. As with atmospheric perspective, selective or variable focus suggests a system for conveying depth in space. Conversely, uniform definition or focus—maximum depth-of-field—denies spatial depth and is a key to two-dimensional flatness in any medium.

Definition and Music

In music, space is articulated in essentially the same way that it is in visual art. The illusion of spatial depth is created by differences in definition or "presence." Sounds of differing amplitude (loudness), pitch or timbre suggest *several* planes in space, creating the basis for spatial or musical depth. Sounds which are of similar amplitude, pitch or timbre suggest a *single* plane in space. As in visual design, uniform definition in music results in an impression of flatness.

There are many ways to structure musical or acoustic space. Harmony itself is largely a spatial device; three-part harmony suggests three levels of space, four-part harmony, four levels. The sensation of space is more or less clear depending on the harmonic intervals between the notes; for example, sevenths and ninths are less certain spatially than thirds and fifths. But the most basic means of conveying depth in music is probably amplitude or volume. The juxtaposition of loud and soft sounds enables the listener to make judgments about relative location in space: *loud* and *soft* translate readily into *near* and *far.* Although music is generally considered a temporal art form— it occurs in "time,"—it draws much of its expressive strength from its capacity to articulate space.

Presence

We are surrounded by space. We look around us—space extends in every direction. Whether we stand still, walk or drive, we have the impression that we are at its center. Paradoxically, all people share this illusion of spatial centricity and the unique point of view it fosters. The things that we see in space are located at different distances from us—people, cars, buildings, trees, hills, clouds, and so on. In general, things furthest away get the least attention; things closest to us get the most—they have *presence.* In design, events or elements with presence tend to be dominant.

Presence and *definition* are closely connected. Things that have presence, whether they are objects, sounds or elements in a painting, are usually highly defined. They are clear, distinct and easily perceived. On the other hand, things that are off in the distance have relatively low definition; edges become diffuse and contrast low. In daylight, distant images appear lighter, with an apparent loss of clarity. Atmospheric perspective incorporates this principle, providing a method for illustrating spatial depth.

Another factor which strongly influences presence is color. Pure, fully saturated color has more presence than tinted or diluted color. Warm colors have more presence than cool colors, light colors more than dark ones. The familiar sight of a blue haze on distant mountains shows us that color gets cooler as things are further away, largely due to the intervening atmosphere.

Presence and Music

In music, presence is a characteristic of high fidelity recording. Today, it is routinely achieved in recording studios by sound engineers using extremely discrete microphones and sophisticated electronic equipment. Music with presence contains a full range of frequencies faithfully reproduced at relatively high amplitude. For the listener, this creates a feeling of "being there" listening to live music. A simple analogy tells us that if a sound with presence has a full range of frequencies (high, middle and low), then an image with presence has a full range of densities (light, middle-gray and dark).

In synthesizing sound, presence is sometimes heightened by emphasizing high and low frequencies while reducing middle frequencies. This results in increased auditory contrast and a sharpening of perception. Similarly, presence in images may be enhanced by reducing the middle-gray tones and stressing the contrast between light and dark. In the sixteenth century, Caravaggio employed this method in his naturalistic, religious canvases. It was called *chiaroscuro,* meaning "light and dark."

Condition

Complete and Incomplete Information

The organization of information into relationships, patterns and wholes is a vital aspect of our cognitive process. It is a creative, synthesizing activity, often considered a measure of human intelligence. When we encounter information that is in some way incomplete, we will frequently supply the missing parts or pieces ourselves. Psychologists call this kind of audience participation *filling-in,* or making *closure.*

Dick Blanchard
Tiger
Gouache on bristol

Closure

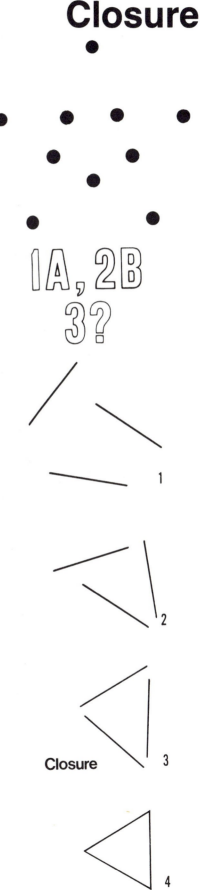

Closure is involved in the perception of shape. An enclosed, framed or bounded shape is readily distinguishable from its field; thus, it is more likely to attract attention. The stars in the sky create an undifferentiated field, but once we notice the Big Dipper, it stands out as a distinct and separate pattern—a constellation.

When ancient astrologers plotted lions and scorpions in the sky, they were motivated by the same psychological need to make closure as children playing follow the dots in a riddle book. Filling-in is one of the more pleasurable aspects of being human and one of the more important. We learn better when we are participating. Every school teacher knows that an active audience is an attentive one. We listen better, notice more and remember longer when we are involved; the transaction of information seems more relevant and meaningful. The experience is more enjoyable.

In the wilderness, many animals mark, occupy and defend an area of land as a territory. Although the borders of such territories may be imperceptible to humans, they are quite real and vivid to other animals. Naturalists' studies of animal behavior in the wild have shown that territory is invariably tied to aggression and dominance. In a sense, animal territories are much like sketched shapes or stellar constellations—closure is a question of perception.

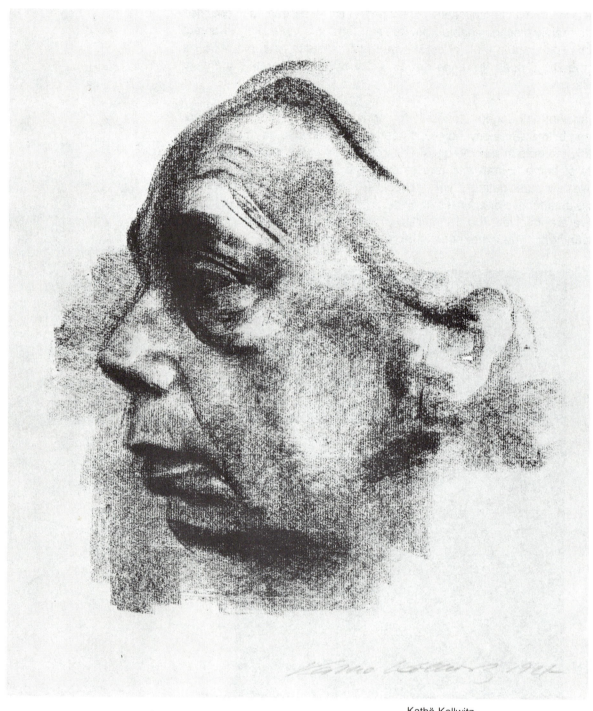

Kathë Kollwitz
Self Portrait in Profile (1927)
Lithograph
Bequest of W.G. Russell Allen
Courtesy, Museum of Fine Arts, Boston

(*above*) Thomas Eakins
Walt Whitman
Oil on panel. 5¼ × 5¼ in.
Helen and Alice Colburn Fund
Courtesy, Museum of Fine Arts, Boston

(*right*) Georges de la Tour
The Repentant Magdalen
Oil on canvas. 44½ × 36½ in.
Ailsa Mellon Bruce Fund 1974
National Gallery of Art, Washington, D.C.

Frames

Frames and Fields

The most elementary act of organization that can be called a design is the simple, bounded field. A boundless field, if one can imagine such a thing, is not a design but rather an abstract state or condition. A field must be bounded or framed in some way in order to be differentiated. Once bounded, the perimeter or edge constitutes an event which defines the limits of the field and makes it meaningful. The work of Jackson Pollock illustrates this well. His dripped and splattered paintings are complex, organic fields bounded by a simple, geometric frame. The frame is the event.

Furthermore, it can be deduced that all paintings, drawings and photographs are bounded fields and that the field and its perimeter or frame constitute the prime field-event relationship. This has led some painters to propose that the act of framing is itself the key conceptual activity in art. For these painters, what is "in" the painting—its content—is of little interest.

Finally, there is a perceptible principle couched in the relation between field and frame—the simpler the field, the greater the importance of the frame and conversely, the more complex the field, the less important the frame.

Jackson Pollock
Autumn Rhythm
Oil on canvas. 105 × 207 in.
Metropolitan Museum of Art, New York
George A. Hearn Fund, 1957

Sixteenth Century Persian Miniature
Bahram Gur in the Turquoise Palace on Wednesday
Metropolitan Museum of Art
Gift of Alexander Smith Cochran, 1913

Frames

Books, tabletops, televisions, windows, postcards, maps, flags and faces are all *frames.* Their primary function is to focus and fix attention. It follows that *framing* and *focusing* are closely related and that both are antithetical to *scanning.* Furthermore, framing is an act of differentiation; when something is framed, it is separated from its environment—its field. It gains notice and becomes an event; its value increases. In general, framing is a prelude to dominance.

Sculpture

Sculpture—design in three dimensions—shares much in common with two-dimensional or pictorial design and follows the same organizational patterns and principles. The edges or borders of a sculpture may be compared to the borders or frame of a painting. If the sculpture is simple, as in the work of Henry Moore or David Smith, the value of contour or sculptural frame is increased; it gets more attention. Conversely, if the sculpture is complex, the value of contour and frame decreases; the stress falls on interior plastic development, as in the work of Bernini or Louise Nevelson.

The relationship between contour—sculptural frame—and interior—sculptural mass—constitutes a primary field-event relationship and is characterized by the usual pattern of hierarchy and dominance, that is, one of the two (contour or interior) tends to be dominant.

As discussed previously, dominance is a feature of field-event relationships in either two or three dimensions. However, like paintings, sculpture may also be designed on the organizational model of fields. Such works do not display dominance but rather an overall sense of harmony and concord. All parts and aspects are of more or less equal importance—we are encouraged to scan; our attention is diffused.

In sculpture, the field is moveable rather than static or fixed. Even in so-called permanent installations, sculpture is often at the mercy of changing environments. but when it is moved, the consequences are dramatic. Sculpture in a garden is perceived differently than sculpture in a primordial rain forest or sculpture in a penthouse gallery. Our perception of an event is always tied to the field in which it occurs. Thus, an Oceanic mask in an urban museum takes on new and different dimensions of meaning, just as Henry Moore's sculpture would be perceived differently in a Samoan fishing village. Ironically, paintings, drawings and photographs are less vulnerable to movement or changing environments; they carry their fields with them, inside their undetachable borders—their frames.

Beginning with the Classical Age of Greece some 2,500 years ago, sculpture acquired an identity and purpose of its own, slowly freeing itself from the old, stone grasp of architecture. In this newfound freedom was born the traditional

Western notion that sculpture is self-contained, independent of its time and place. Two thousand years later, the Italian Renaissance fulfilled that promise of freedom; sculpture had become high art. No longer did it serve its old master, architecture; indeed, Michelangelo's monumental statues seem oddly indifferent to their architectural settings, even when they adorn de Medici's Tomb. Three hundred and fifty years later still, Rodin's bronzes stand heroically alone, their independence an accomplished fact. However, in his unfinished masterpiece, *The Gates of Hell,* Rodin seems to make a faintly melancholy gesture to the old partnership between sculpture and architecture, but now the roles are reversed: Rodin uses the architectural framework the way a painter would use canvas—as a ground to support and organize his figures.

Auguste Rodin
The Thinker
Bronze
National Gallery of Art, Washington, D.C.
Gift of Mrs. John W. Simpson 1942

Louise Nevelson
Sky Cathedral
Museum of Modern Art, New York

Today, we have come full circle. Many contemporary sculptors strive to transcend the classical notion that art is self-contained, aloof from its environment. Rather, they design projects for specific sites, with appropriate research and planning, to ensure that their works relate directly to their environments. They often involve community groups as well as co-artists in both the preparation and the building of the project, restoring the old communal quality of the art experience. Smithson and Christo are two of the more spectacular advocates of this approach, conspicuous because of the grand scale of their public artworks. But there is a private, personal side to this approach as well: It expresses the artist's human need to make meaningful, rewarding connections with the world in which he or she lives.

In conceptual or environmental art, the environment is the field; the sculptural object or event, whatever it may be, is the event. Together they form an archetypal field-event relationship.

Robert I. Katz
The Meeting Place

Conceptual works stressing "performance" bridge the gap
between traditional theater and the plastic arts.

Richard Blanchard
Primatec

Photos by Bruce Armstrong

Photos by Jere De Waters

Sasson Soffer
Amen

(*below*) Sasson Soffer
Morriah

(*right*) Thomas Goyla
Untitled

(*below right*) *Statue of Djed-Ptuh-Iuf-Ankh*
Egyptian, Late Dynasty 25
Red quartzite block, 26.7 cm.
Gift of Mr. and Mrs. Donald Edgar
through the Egyptian Curator's Fund
Courtesy, Museum of Fine Arts, Boston

102

Io, one of Jupiter's
several moons.
Courtesy, NASA

*In nature, forms are shaped and
"framed" by their environments,
much as they are in art. The
"form–environment" correlation is
part of a larger spectrum of field-
event relationships in general.*

Photo by Ron Crosley

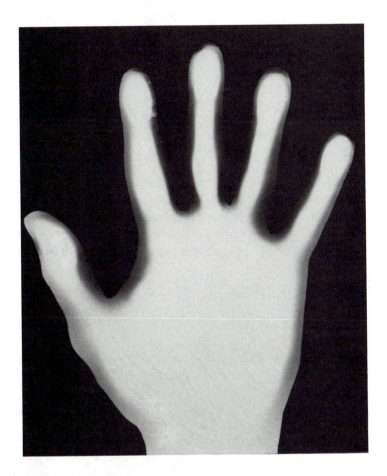

Number

In the analysis of field-event relationships, the *number* of events is a central consideration. Some designs are simple, containing only one event. Others are very complicated, involving many events. Understandably, the more events there are, the more complicated the task of organizing them becomes. But that is not all; number also affects value. The more events in a field, the less attention any one event receives; its relative value is diminished. Number is an aspect of form; quantity, amount, ratio, proportion and number are innate in the structure of all art.

Let's consider some of the more common numbers in the context of field-event theory.

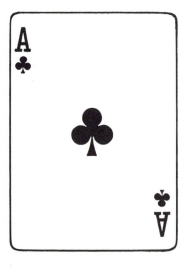

One

1

When there is one event in a field, the problem is simple. The field is usually negative, the event positive: it is an either-or situation. The event is guaranteed full attention, and its value is correspondingly high. It readily assumes dominance. Designs with one event often convey a monumental simplicity and directness. For this reason, they tend to have great expressive power.

James McNeill Whistler
The White Girl (Symphony in White No. 1)
Harris Whittmore Collection
National Gallery of Art, Washington, D.C.

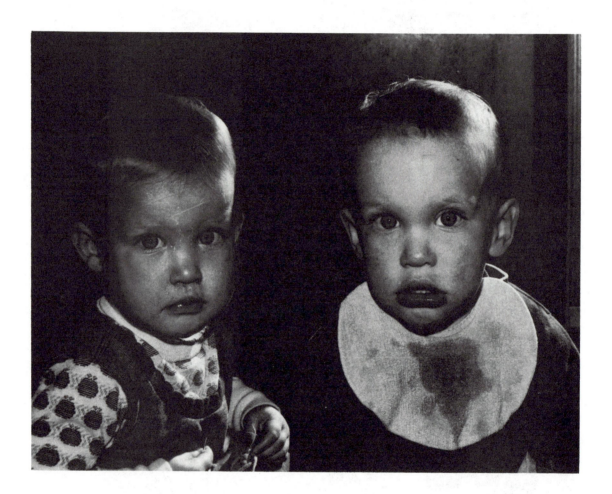

2

Two

When there are two events in a field, there are at least two possibilities:

1. **If the events are identical or similar and the distance between them is less than the distance between any one of them and the edge of the field, they will form a pair and *act as one*. An identical pair, "twins," dominates the field in much the same way that one event does.**

2. **If two events do not form a pair, they set up a typical hierarchical relationship—one is dominant, the other subdominant or subordinate. The subdominant event is called a *secondary event,* the dominant event is a *primary event.***

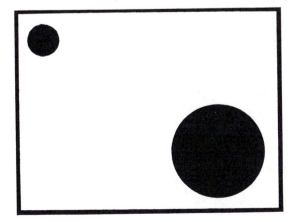 

2

The importance of two cannot be overestimated. We are bipedal, binocular organisms. We perceive our world with the aid of matrices based on two, that is, polar pairs such as "yes" and "no," "up" and "down," or "light" and "dark." Our computers run on binary systems; so does mating and marriage.

Two's place in the world is secure. It is the second most popular number. Its ancestry is ancient and its history lavish. It is not, however, without its shady side. The number two seems to have a unique potential for tension. Explorers embarking on long expeditions know that a two-man party is likely to develop unmanageable tensions and so a three-man party is generally preferred. Some anthropologists believe that human progress really began when human beings stood up on their hind legs, freeing their hands to explore, hold, manipulate and, eventually, make tools. It seems, however, that two hands are almost too much. Nature, well-versed in the parlance of competition, solved the problem neatly by making one hand dominant—most of us are right-handed. Similarly, two events in a field tend to compete and conflict unless one is clearly dominant or distinctly different.

Three

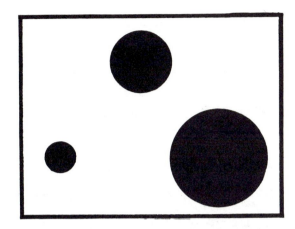 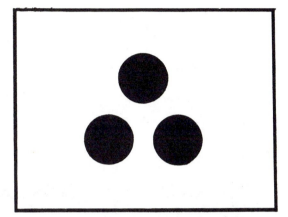

When there are three events in a field, a shift occurs toward pattern and configuration. It takes three events or elements to make a pattern, just as it takes three tones to make a chord. The importance of three in design is graphically demonstrated by the compositional triangle, as viable today as it was a thousand years ago. The "golden" triangle of the Pythagoreans, the Renaissance triangle used by Leonardo da Vinci and the structural triangle of Buckminster Fuller are stately variations on the theme of three. Similarly, Egypt's monumental pyramids and Christianity's Holy Trinity testify to three's universal spiritual significance.

Pyramids of Mycerinus, Chephren and Cheops
Courtesy of the American Museum of Natural History, New York

More Than Three

When the number of events exceeds three, options multiply dramatically. We are faced with the formidable challenge of organizing many events into patterns or configurations which structure and unify the whole. To this end, the artist may explore layers or networks of patterns, just as the astronomer explores constellations within galaxies. Such designs are highly complex, although great artists often make them appear simple. It is a safe guess that quantity and complexity go hand in hand, both in natural and man-made design.

John Singer Sargent
The Daughters of Edward D. Boit
Oil on canvas. 221 × 221 cm.
Gift of Mary Louisa Boit, Florence D. Boit, Jane Hubbard Boit, and Julia Overing Boit in memory of their father
Courtesy, Museum of Fine Arts, Boston

Jim Dine
Five Paint Brushes
Etching. 35½ × 23½ in.
Gift of the Print and Drawing Club
Courtesy, Museum of Fine Arts, Boston

In American popular art and folklore, our heroes are one of a kind: there is only one Wonder Woman, one Superman, one Kojak and one Elvis. Their command of the field is total. They are not merely dominant, they are unbeatable. Apparently, we find it gratifying to focus all our attention on one dazzling event. Heroes also come in pairs, but the partners are rarely identical or equal. The Lone Ranger and Tonto, Don Quixote and Sancho Panza, Abbott and Costello, and Batman and Robin typify heroic or comic pairs. Predictably, the "dynamic duo" is dominance-oriented, stressing a dominant character over a subordinate. The success of such duos always lies in the exaggerated contrast between the two characters. Heroic trios are uncommon, as are comic trios, although the Three Musketeers and the Three Stooges enjoyed modest successes. Trios are more common in music, and will occasionally take on a mythic power usually reserved for one-of-a-kind soloists. Jimi Hendrix overwhelmed audiences with his authoritative three-man format, but it was the quartet, popularized by the Beatles, that became the unofficial model for rock bands in the sixties and seventies.

Groups of four, five or six are true bands, acting as a unit for their mutual advantage, as did archaic hunting bands in prehistoric times. Bands of a dozen or more become "big bands" or orchestras and, while they may sometimes feature a soloist, they are generally made up of more or less anonymous, interchangeable members. At this size, band leaders become necessary. A symphony orchestra of forty or more members is a corporate structure which acts like a field. It is led by a dominant, often heroic individual—its conductor. The symphony conductor is one of a kind, for more than one would be redundant and disastrous to the music. The conductor stands alone, one event in a field. We have now come full circle in our brief exploration of numbers, returning finally to our first number—one.

(*above*) John Singer Sargent
Rehearsal of the Pasdeloup Orchestra at the Cirque d'Hiver (c. 1876)
Oil on canvas. 55.2 × 46.3 cm.
Charles Henry Hayden Fund
Courtesy, Museum of Fine Arts, Boston

(*right*) James McNeill Whistler
Arrangement in Flesh Color and Black:
Portrait of Theodore Duret (1983)
Oil on canvas. 76½ × 35½ in.
Metropolitan Museum of Art, New York
Wolf Fund, 1913

114

Size

Size involves amount and measurement; it is quantitative and most often expressed by the polar adjectives "large" and "small." Our natural expectation is that large things dominate small ones. Although this is often true, it is far from axiomatic. In design, there are many situations in which a smaller shape attracts more attention and becomes dominant. This is usually determined by the following principle: When the difference between two shapes (one large, one small) is greater than the difference between the larger shape and the field, the smaller shape becomes dominant.

Size is a key factor in the articulation of field-event relationships. When an event (a shape) is more than half as large as the field in which it sits, it becomes field-oriented and begins to lose its identity as an event. Consequently, it ceases to be dominant. In general, a dominant event is less than half the size of its field. (See the "Principle of Unequal Division" on page 47 for a more detailed discussion.)

Of course, size is relative. It acquires meaning through the articulation of differences—sometimes called *scale*. Moreover, it is heavily influenced by other dominance factors such as position, shape, color, contrast and cathexis. Only rarely does size by itself account for dominance.

1

2

3

4

5

6

The diagram above shows six pairs of rectangles. Which pair best illustrates dominance? In which is dominance most uncertain?

Rembrandt van Rijn
Rembrandt Leaning on a Stone Sill
Etching
Harvey D. Parker Collection
Courtesy, Museum of Fine Arts, Boston

Position

Position

In any field certain positions tend to be dominant. In two-dimensional design, upper-left and bottom-right are dominant positions, stemming in part from our reading and writing habits. But the most important position is probably the center. It provides a natural focal point which is stable, balanced and orderly. Symbolically, the center is the "heart."

On the social ladder, elevation is a vital factor. To be higher often means to be better. Neither education nor revolution will eradicate the expression "upper class" or the notion that heaven is "up" and hell is "down." Similarly, the home, church or castle on the hilltop will always dominate both the landscape and our attention.

Introductions and first impressions are important in many situations, such as at job interviews and opening nights. And being first is often associated with being best. But in much dramatic literature and cinema, the last act—the climax—is dominant.

Position is as important in the hierarchy of design as it is in social hierarchies. To many people, being in the right place at the right time is the key to success. It is also the key to good design.

Our sense of position in space relies heavily on a scale of polarized terms such as "up-down," "high-low" and "north-south." Each pair of opposing terms is a matrix, a kind of womb in which meaning is shaped. Thus we are able to make judgments about relative position and direction. Shape acquires meaning in the same way. In defiance of common sense, such basic shapes as circles and squares tend to lose meaning when positioned alone. Even the simplest shapes acquire meaning only when perceived in terms of polar relationships. In *Art and Visual Perception,* Rudolf Arnheim explains that "only when other shapes, e.g. straight lines or squares, have become artic-ulated, do round shapes begin to stand for roundness: heads, the sun, palms of hands." He further states, "A circle is a circle only when triangles are available as an alternative." Arnheim reached these conclusions by his thoughtful study of children's art. However, what he ascertains by experiment, we can confirm by personal experience; we all have access to the same information.

Winslow Homer
The Fog Warning
Otis Norcross Fund, Gift of
Miss Laura and Grenville H. Norcross
Oil on canvas. 76.2 × 121.6 cm.

COLOR

The Color Wheel

It has long been known that white light contains all the colors of the rainbow and that these colors can be separated and made visible with a prism, yielding a spectrum. This spectrum can be bent into a circle to produce a color wheel. The illustration below shows that the color wheel is usually divided into twelve parts or chromatic steps. There are three primary colors, making a triad of red, yellow and blue; three secondaries, making a triad of orange, green and violet; and six tertiary colors.

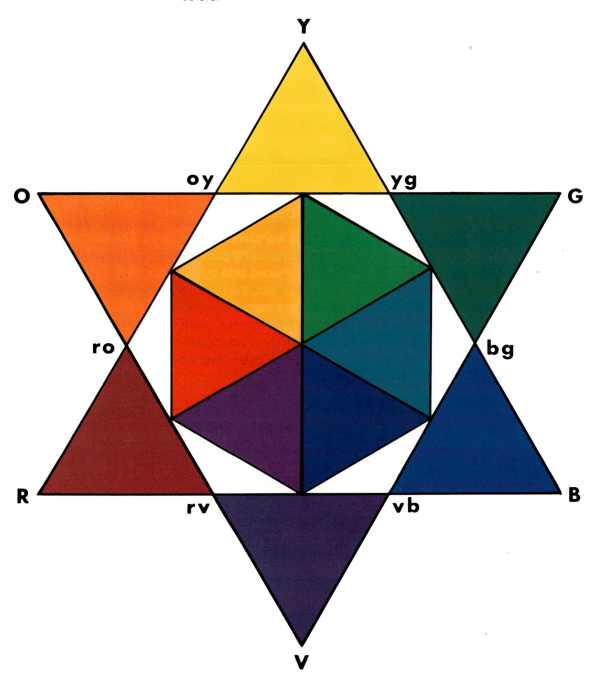

126

Warm and Cool Color

The color wheel may be bisected into a "warm" half and a "cool" half. Convention dictates that hues oriented toward red and yellow are considered warm; those toward blue are cool. The overall "temperature" of a painting, or any work of art that involves color, is a vital factor in design, both in terms of structure and in terms of expression. It is particularly important that temperature ambiguity be avoided by making one of the two (warm or cool) dominant. Equal amounts of warm and cool color will sometimes cancel each other, resulting in the deterioration of chromatic quality and causing "muddy" color. On the other hand, the interplay of warm and cool can also result in the intensification of color sensation and chromatic luminosity, as demonstrated in the works of the French Impressionists.

Harmony and Contrast

Harmony and *contrast* represent the two basic ways in which color relationships may be established. Hues adjacent to each other on the color wheel are called analogous, suggesting that they are closely related through similarity or harmony. A group of analogous colors, sometimes called a *family,* provides the simplest form of color harmony.

Hues opposite each other on the color wheel are called complements and are characterized by contrast. Precise complements yield maximum color differentiation and contrast. Color contrast may also be developed in terms of value or intensity, leading to a virtually infinite variety of chromatic combinations.

Courtesy of NASA

Reflection and Absorption

The color of an object is the result of its function of reflection and absorption of light. An object which reflects all of the light reaching it appears white; one which absorbs all of the light appears black. An object which absorbs some wavelengths of light but reflects others appears colored. An apple, for example, absorbs all wavelengths except one—red. Similarly, all wavelengths of light normally pass through the sky, except blue, which is reflected by the atmosphere. This suggests that color is not an intrinsic attribute of objects but rather the result of their differing reflection and absorption patterns.

Spatial-Kinetic Characteristics of Color

All colors have specific spatial-kinetic characteristics; they either advance or recede in space, relative to each other and to the viewer. In general, warm, brilliant and saturated colors advance, appearing closer to us; cool, dull and unsaturated colors recede, appearing more distant. This suggests that a color composition is also a spatial-kinetic code; each and every color is a cue to a specific position in space, actual or pictorial. This is also the key principle of the spectrograph, used by astronomers to determine the relative position and motion of stars deep in interstellar space. The spectrograph divides the light received from a star into separate wavelengths, each of which produces a different color. Arranged on a line, these colors form a spectrum. Theoretically, every star in the universe has its own spectrum, depending on where it is and which way it is moving. Scientists analyze spectrums for their *red* or *blue shift* (Doppler effect). A shift towards red means the star is receding relative to earth; a shift away from red means it is advancing. This spatial-kinetic color code enables the astronomer to create a "picture" of the cosmos. Similarly, artists use color codes to organize and design pictorial space.

Atmospheric perspective refers to the increasingly bluish appearance of things as they recede into the distance, primarily the result of the intervening atmosphere. A red house on a distant hill seems closer than a blue one. The horizon at sunset, with its warm glow, seems closer to us than it does at noon.

Another important spatial-kinetic characteristic of color is its tendency to expand and contract. In general, warm, bright or light colors expand, appearing larger; cool, dull or dark ones contract, appearing smaller. Thus, a red circle appears larger than a blue one even though they may actually be the same size. Understandably, expansion is often, though not always, associated with dominance.

If color can be coded to structure space and the illusion of "depth," it can also be used to do the reverse: flatten space and deny depth. Indeed, the major thrust of "modern art" has been to reassert the archaic two-dimensional flatness of the picture plane. In the Post-Impressionist period, Henri Matisse challenged color's traditional role of subservience to three-dimensional illusory space, using it more abstractly in terms of its spatial-kinetic characteristics (properties). Later on, in the forties and fifties, Abstract Expressionists released color from all ties with objects and space. Its subservience ended; it was abruptly made king: color itself became the primary point of painting. Today, however, as our understanding of perception and communication continues to improve, color is being thoughtfully reintegrated into design—not as "king," but as a resourceful member of the royal family of arts and crafts.

Functions

Color pervades our world. It is so fundamental to our concept of life that we can scarcely imagine a world without it. To be colorful is to be vital and lively; conversely, the absence of color denotes gloom and lifelessness. But color's importance is more than symbolic; in both culture and nature, color performs a multitude of functions.

In culture, color is an integral part of visual communication on many levels. It is a primary piece of data in identification, e.g., a red house or a blue car. It is used in national symbols such as flags for its power to convey a Gestalt-like corporate message. The restrained blue and white flag of the Finns expresses something quite different from the bold red flag of the Russians or the highly charged red, white and blue of the United States. On streets and highways, traffic lights control endless streams of cars, trucks and pedestrians simply by changing colors. In dress, color is often an index to age group, ethnic background, social lexicon, lifestyle and personality. To the computer programmer, it is "information"; to the psychologist, it is "data"; to the municipal engineer, it is "communication." To the artist, it is a dynamic mode of expression which may be used scientifically, symbolically or poetically to articulate ideas and feelings. Its potential is inexhaustible. Little wonder that, for many people, color is virtually synonymous with art.

Some of nature's most dazzling color is found in flowers. Their brilliant and delicate hues delight the eye and soothe the spirit. We use them to beautify our homes and institutions, embellish our rituals, express love or sympathy or congratulate achievement. However, the color of flowers has neither decorative nor symbolic value in nature; it is simply a matter of survival. Violets, roses, daisies, daffodils and dandelions all rely on their color to attract bees and other insects that will pollinate and so proliferate and perpetuate their kind. Nature's palette may be exquisite, but first it is functional.

In the animal world, color is functional. It plays a vital role in visual signaling and communication between members of the same species and is especially important in identification, territoriality, courting and mating. Among many species of birds, the male has the dual tasks of selecting a territory and attracting a mate. He accomplishes these tasks with the help of two different modes of signaling—song and color. In *Animal Communication,* Hubert Frings explains that "in sexual selection, a female bird selects the most distinct, the loudest, the brightest male." Once the male has established a territory and has attracted a mate, his attention turns to maintenance and defense and, here again, color is called into service. The male bird's colorfulness makes him very conspicuous to his neighbors, which may reduce the possibility of territorial conflict; if he maintains a high profile, other males will be less likely to impinge upon his territory, either by error or intent. In this way, the higher goal of the proper distribution of individuals is also served, enhancing the prospects for survival of the species.

Like birds, fish also employ color for communication in a wide range of areas, including identification, territoriality and courtship. Some use it to catch their dinner, making themselves into enticing lures; others use it to avoid becoming someone else's dinner, adopting the colors of their environment for camouflage. Fish in the tropics are often fantastically colorful, perhaps to take advantage of the high visibility of tropical waters. Not only birds and fish, but insects, reptiles and amphibians also use color for intraspecific communication. Frings writes that "male salamanders of many species are brightly colored and display their colors to court the females."

If color gives the male bird, fish or salamander a competitive edge over his fellows, it does so with a certain amount of risk; it makes him more conspicuous to potential predators—exemplifying nature's system of checks and balances at work. The same is true in art. Color easily gains the viewers attention, but does not guarantee his understanding or appreciation. The artist must use color expressively and intelligently within an aesthetic system of checks and balances to engender communication and strengthen design.

Temperature

In photography, there is a direct correlation between light, color and temperature. The basic principle is that as temperature rises, color changes; it modulates from red to orange, to yellow, to white and, lastly, to blue. This makes it possible to consider color an index to temperature. Color temperature is expressed in Kelvin degrees; candlelight is rated at 1900°K, tungsten light at 3200 to 3400°K and standard daylight at 5500°K (between 10:00 a.m. and 2:00 p.m.). Manufacturers rate their films in terms of sensitivity (speed) and temperature; photographers then select the film that matches the approximated temperature of the light conditions in which they will be shooting. This enables the photographer to achieve reasonably good color balance (color as the eye perceives it) in most situations.

Scientists employ a similar correlation between color and temperature in studying stars. They theorize that stars go through stages of development during which they either expand or contract. A *red giant* is a star that has expanded to enormous size, hundreds of times larger than our sun. Although it is very bright because of the great quantity of light it emits, its temperature is relatively low (3000°C); its color is reddish. As stars age, they contract and their temperatures rise. A *white dwarf* is a star that has contracted to a fraction of its original size; its temperature is high (10,000 to 20,000°C); its color is bluish.

In science and technology, color and temperature are closely related. Every welder knows that the hottest part of the torch flame is the blue tip. However, in the visual arts, convention dictates that red is warm and blue is cool. The meanings of the terms *warm* and *cool* often depend upon the context in which they are used.

Indeed, touch and temperature seem to go hand in hand. When objects rub against each other, whether they are grinding plates in the earth's mantle or a couple of sticks in a boy's hand, friction occurs, causing a rise in temperature. Generally, wherever there is movement, there is heat. Physical exercise, such as jogging or tennis, creates body heat which is released, in part, as perspiration. On the molecular level, heat generates movement among molecules and causes expansion and other chemical changes. It is quite apparent, then, that temperature, touch and movement are closely related in the physical world.

Studies of insect behavior show that there is sometimes a correlation between sound and temperature. Frings notes that "an American grasshopper, Neoconcephalus ensiger, almost doubles the rate of singing for every 10°C rise in temperature." This is due to the fact that the muscles which produce the sound work faster in higher temperatures. On this basis, it is possible to project that sound, like color, is an index to temperature. The rich sensory experience of listening to music may involve tactile warm–cool sensitivities, stimulated by the underlying relation of pitch, tempo, and temperature. Correlations between temperature, color, movement, space, and sound may help explain the extraordinary evocative power of music, a power that has intrigued philosophers and poets throughout the ages.

Finally, temperature has some familiar emotional connotations. Heat is associated with passion, involvement and life; cold with detachment and death. Each of the four seasons carries its own emotional charge—cathexis—that is tied to changes in temperature. Similarly, each of the earth's climatic zones, from the arctic to the equator, may possess its own temperature-related cathexis.

In traditional Japanese Haiku, a form of "linked poetry," it is customary to include a reference to a season, sometimes called a "season-word." The season-word is densely packed with meaning: it evokes a multitude of sights, sounds, smells and tactile sensations (temperature). Moreover, it is a poetic device through which the Haiku poet expresses feelings about life, time's passage and the universal patterns of nature. The season-word carries a high degree of cathexis. (See Cathexis, page 163).

> The wintery gust:
> It blows the evening sun down
> Into the ocean

> Natsume Sōseki
> *Modern Japanese Haiku*
> *An Anthology*

Orientation

The spatial orientation of an event is determined by its relation to the field or frame in which it is located. Its orientation in relation to other events in the same field determines its capacity for dominance. For example, if a group of small rectangles is oriented so that their sides are all parallel to those of the field, then they share a similar orientation. However, if one of the rectangles is made oblique, it is immediately noticed and becomes dominant. Reversing this scenario would have the same result—the event with dissimilar orientation would stand out. In the same way, a group of events equidistant from each other share a common spatial orientation. If one of them is moved further away, it usually attracts more attention and becomes dominant in the design. It is evident that dissimilarity is a key factor in both these examples of orientation.

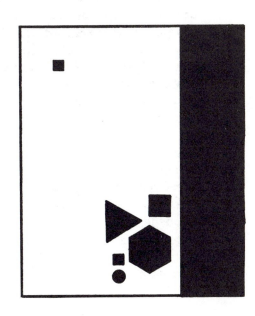

Motion

Animation is commonly considered a sign of life. All living things move or have moving parts, internally or externally. The heart beats, blood circulates, veins pulse and nerves twitch; for all but the most accomplished yogi, there is no such thing as standing still. Vision itself involves continuous movement; rods and cones, the light receptors in the eye, are in a state of perpetual vibration. Furthermore, our most basic visual activity is scanning. Our eyes constantly scan, roam and probe the visual field, holding only a pinpoint in focus at any given instant. Our predilection for movement makes it a dominance factor of major importance.

Implied or actual motion naturally attracts and commands attention. Our eyes involuntarily follow movement; it is an automatic reflex. To a cat, movement means a possible meal—it becomes instantaneously alert and poised to stalk and charge. Most animals are keenly sensitive to movement, for their lives often depend on their ability to detect it and react. The quicker their reaction, the better their chances for survival. On the other hand, perfect stillness—the "freezing" of frogs or chipmunks—is a ploy to escape notice, that is, to attract *no* attention.

Philip Paratore
Winter Woods Series
Oil on canvas paper. 16 × 20 in.

Motion

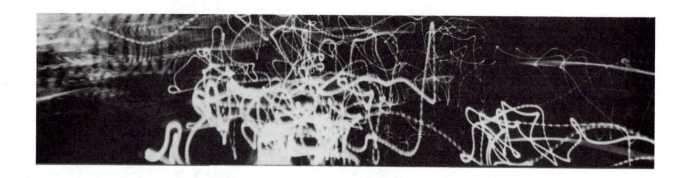

Ming Dynasty Calligraphy
Album Leaf
John Ware Willard Fund
Courtesy, Museum of Fine Arts, Boston

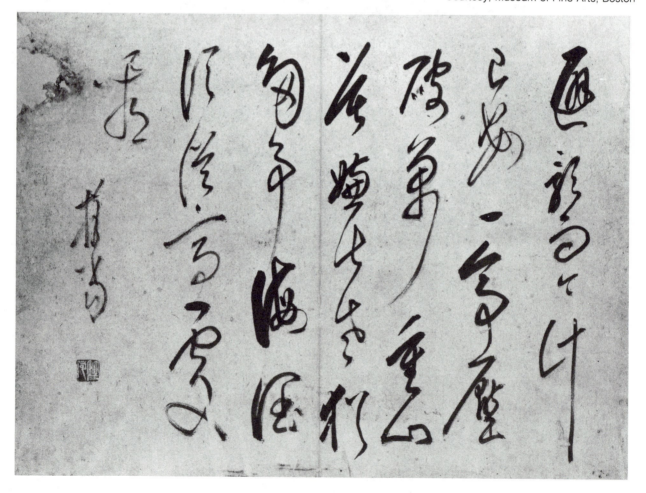

Direction

Where there is movement, there is direction. In general, movement through time and space implies direction even when no destination is in sight; all that is needed is a frame of reference. In, fact, direction is meaningful only in relation to a reference point or constant position; a car moves from right to left when we stand on one side of the road and from left to right when we stand on the other. Similarly, the directional movement of the earth would be imperceptible without the moon, sun and stars as reference points.

In and out, up and down, coming and going, advancing and receding, expanding and contracting are typical adjectives that describe direction. Although there is no such thing as a purely dominant direction, movement that leads to or from a dominant position often becomes dominant. Paradoxically, direction and position are antithetical; direction implies movement while position implies fixity.

Shape

Shape is often defined as enclosed space or area. It is usually associated with and influenced by other factors such as size, position, definition, dissimilarity and cathexis. Despite this apparent relativity, some shapes display dominance. Geometric shapes tend to dominate organic ones; highly defined, hard-edged shapes dominate soft shapes; angular dominates curved and convex dominates concave. Some shapes get more attention because they are easier to perceive or more stimulating to the senses. For example, shapes with sharp edges or points (triangles, diamonds, stars) actively engage our visual, tactile and kinetic sensitivities and have psychological overtones as well. They may subliminally translate into archetypal mountain peaks, daggers or canine teeth, all of which carry high amounts of cathexis. Angles pierce space and suggest outward movement; they are aggressive, not passive. A diamond-shaped painting needs more wall space than a rectangular one. Circles, on the other hand, are self-contained and relatively harmonious. Curves suggest accord, angles discord. Interestingly enough, Buckminster Fuller's geodesic dome combines the triangle and the circle to make a structure of exceptional tensile strength and aesthetic beauty. In synthesized music, angular waveforms such as the sawtooth assault the ear, demanding our attention. But the smoothly curved "sine" wave is calm and undemanding, like the circle. The sine is also the simplest waveform, suggesting an inverse relationship between simplicity and intensity in sensory perception. It is an easy sound to listen to.

The five-pointed star is a group of angles arranged around the edge of a circle. It graphically combines excitement and stability, making it well-suited for the expression of patriotic or nationalistic themes. It is not surprising that many national flags incorporate the star. The Japanese flag, however, uses a perfectly proportioned red circle in a white rectangular field, suggesting serenity and strength.

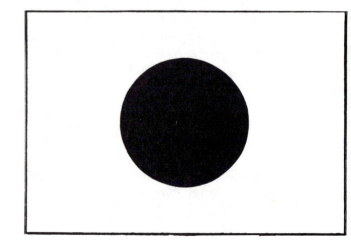

Photo by Dorothy Pepe

Thirty spokes share the wheel's hub;
It is the center hole that makes it useful.
Shape clay into a vessel;
It is the space within that makes it useful.
Cut doors and windows for a room;
It is the holes which make it useful.
Therefore profit comes from what is there;
Usefulness from what is not there.

Lao Tsu
Sixth Century B.C.

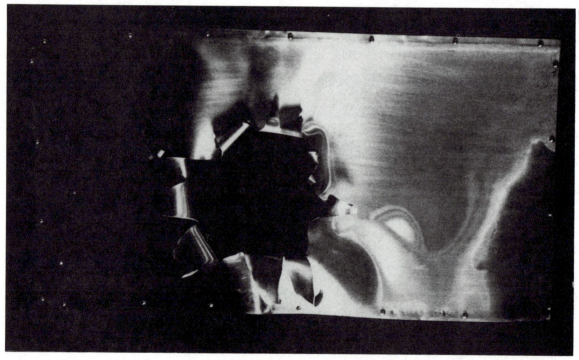

Michael Woods
Exploded Steel

Negative-Positive Shape

Figure—ground relationships consist of a negative and a positive component. In visual design, these are called positive and negative shapes, and the way they fit together is the heart of composition. Our natural tendency is to interpret *figure* as positive, *ground* as negative. But this interpretation is by no means sacred. Artists have been manipulating negative—positive assignations in painting for over three quarters of a century, led, perhaps, by the influential French painter Henri Matisse. Today, the study of negative and positive shape is a central part of every design curriculum.

Positive shape normally receives more attention than negative shape, although both are vital in design. We naturally associate positive shape with an object—person or teapot, moon or mountain. In general, objects dominate space, positive dominates negative, figure dominates ground and events dominate fields.

Photography is a medium that naturally increases our awareness of the plastic relation between positive and negative. Any seasoned photographer will tell you that a good print begins with a good negative. In fact, much of photography involves the study of negatives from both a technical and aesthetic standpoint to determine their image-yielding qualities. Unlike artists in most other visual mediums, the photographer routinely works with two sets of information, a negative and a positive. This experience has a distinct advantage—it encourages sensitivity to wholes and the way that they are formed by positive and negative components.

Impressionist painters minimized negative—positive differentiation, creating instead unified fields with a maximum of positivity. This later led to the notion of setting everything on one picture plane and the evolution of an aesthetic movement based on flatness, which dominated painting for the first half of the twentieth century. Of course, the primacy of the flat surface could only be maintained by the formal denial of spatial depth in painting.

It is almost as though the illusion of depth had to be dispensed with so that it could be rebuilt again in modern, plastic terms. This perhaps was the mission of Cubism, engineered by Picasso and Braque. However, the flattening of the picture plane has been instructive, for it reveals much about vision. It shows that our depth perception relies heavily on visual cues originating in figure—ground relationships and that this perception is greatly enhanced by maximizing negative—positive differentiation.

Norman Therrien
Bronze Figure

Sculpture is one of the world's oldest art forms, strong in traditions and historicity. And yet, it is not always well understood. Sculpture is design in three dimensions, sharing the usual aesthetic concern for the relation between positive and negative. However, this relation is not always apparent. There is a natural emphasis on the positive, perhaps because most sculptures are free-standing objects, easily read as figures. The negative space within and around a sculpture is intangible and unseen, elusive to the viewer, who is more inclined to focus attention on the sculptural object itself. Here, then, lies the challenge—sculpture in the round seems not to have a ground. But, in fact, the space in which the sculpture stands is the ground. It is only because this space is not clearly bounded or framed in any way that it eludes our notice and is discounted. All sculptors know that the design of negative and positive is as important in their art form as it is in any other.

The work of Henry Moore is remarkable in its imaginative reinterpretation of positive and negative in sculpture. His monumental figures often contain gaping holes and sloping concavities set against massive, convex forms. The effect is one of immense plastic vitality, a vitality that characterizes the best modern art.

Negative–positive dynamics are equally vital in music. The composer in any genre—pop, rock, jazz or classical—is a designer of space and silence; the interval or space between notes and beats is the basis of melody, harmony and rhythm. A musical composition is an arrangement of negative spaces and positive sounds and therefore conforms to the same general principles as any visual composition or design.

Juan Gris
Still Life with Guitar
Oil on canvas. 28½ × 36 in.
Gift of Mr. Joseph Pulitzer, 12/13/67
Courtesy, Museum of Fine Arts, Boston

Henry Moore
Reclining Figure (1951)
Plaster cast
Art Gallery of Ontario, Toronto
Gift of Henry Moore, 1974

Negative and Positive "Social" Space

At present, our culture lacks a philosophical tradition for the articulation of space, as our cities and suburbs with their rampant shopping centers and commercial strips grimly testify. We are object-oriented and share a corporate bias toward the material. As modern populations increase and technology expands, an understanding of negative and positive space becomes more and more crucial. In the absence of tradition, artistic intuition may be our most valuable resource.

Pablo Picasso
Guernica
Oil on canvas. $137\frac{1}{2} \times 305$ in.
© SPADEM, Paris/VAGA, New York 1983

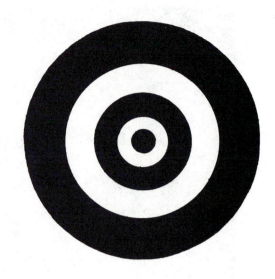

Configuration

It is well-known that some configurations or arrangements have intrinsic attention-getting power. A chief characteristic of such configurations is *convergence*. In general, any convergence of energy or information tends to produce both a focal point and a central position. Events which converge on an actual or implied center—a dart target, a distant star cluster, or our own spiral-shaped Milky Way—create a natural focal point which readily assumes dominance. Just as magnetic lines of force lead us inexorably to a magnet, so convergence always leads us to a dominant center.

Junction, overlap and *interface* are also characterized by convergence. Additionally, they have a strong tendency to emphasize position. For example, a line by itself conveys little information, but crossed with a second line, it becomes a set of coordinates that pinpoint a precise position. Information and action intensify at intersections; see any street corner or railroad crossing for easy verification. In design, visual junctions and intersections stop our scanning eye as surely as red lights stop traffic. Like centers, junctions are naturally dominant in their fields.

Overlap is an interesting but limited case of convergence. If two linear shapes (circles, squares, etc.) partially overlap, the shared area (the overlapped area) tends to be dominant.

Like intersections, interfaces are extremely vital configurations. The study of color theory and sensory perception shows us that the action is always intensified at the edge where two colors meet—the interface. On a larger scale, the interface between cultures, sexes, races, ages or political ideologies tends to be a focus of intense attention.

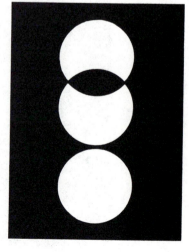

Configuration

Philip Paratore
Hallowell Quarry Series

Convergence

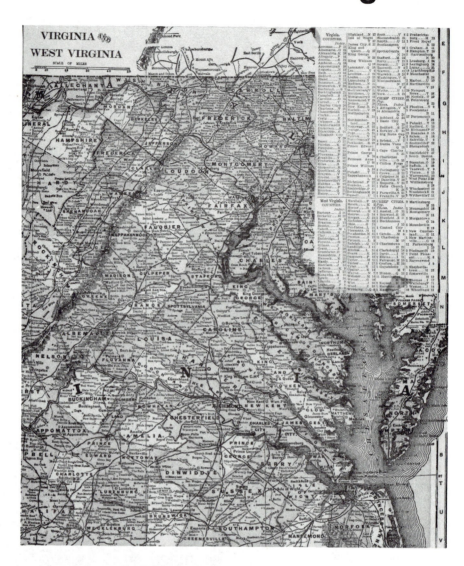

Wherever energy and information converge, the result is centrality and dominance.

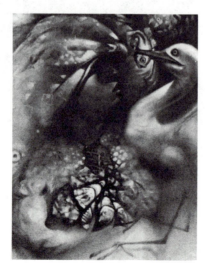

Intersection

The intersection of opposing lines (vertical and horizontal) creates a focal point of great power. It commands the viewer's eye and attention, while at the same time it inhibits casual scanning. The innate focusing power of the intersection is apparent in the traditional Christian symbol, the crucifix.

Joos van Cleef
The Crucifixion
Oil on canvas. 80 × 63.5 cm.
Purchased by the Picture Fund
Courtesy, Museum of Fine Arts, Boston

Systems

Consistent patterns and rhythms tend to generate systems—highly organized configurations.

Simple and Complex Configurations

There is a natural human bias toward simplicity based on the survival value of speed. Simple configurations or arrangements of information can be comprehended faster than complex ones. However, simplicity is a relative term, often subjective, and closely tied to its opposite—complexity. In a complex field, a simple event easily assumes dominance. Conversely, in a simple field, a complex event is dominant.

Complexity is a corollary of convergence. It involves a gathering or accumulation of information. It also involves variety; different kinds of information often combine to produce an impression of complexity.

In contrast to the high-speed scanning and instantaneous gestalts allowed by simple designs, complex designs force us to slow down, get involved, focus our attention and concentrate. Complexity precludes snap judgments or easy answers. Because it often contains large quantities of information—visual or verbal—complexity is both stimulating and demanding; it is the domain of the specialist and the scholar.

Philip Paratore
Deborah Angelica

Symmetry

Courtesy of the American Museum of Natural History, New York

The concept of symmetry is ancient, deriving perhaps from the human body's structure. Our sense of a right and a left side must be at least as old as self-consciousness itself. Further, symmetry is associated with balance, which is, in turn, tied to our bipedal verticality. With roots as deep and distant as these, it is no wonder that symmetry retains its expressive value even today. Major civilizations throughout history have recognized the implicit psychological power of symmetry; examples can be found everywhere. The pyramids of Cheops, the post-and-lintel monuments at Stonehenge, the Taj Mahal, and the Parthenon all employ and enjoy the service of symmetry.

Symmetry is one of the most common configurations in design. Symmetry is based on:

1. **a central axis**
2. **apparent equality on both sides of the axis**
3. **a frame or perimeter**

Symmetry

Symmetry and centrality are closely related; symmetry implies a central axis. But a central axis is difficult to determine without a frame or edge of some kind for reference. Thus, the relation between center and frame is of fundamental importance in symmetry. This makes it ideally suited to national symbols such as flags, for what is a nation if not a central authority with recognized and secured boundaries? For the same reason, symmetrical designs are also common in corporate symbols—trademarks, letterheads, and logos.

Both centrality and symmetry stress position rather than movement. They tend to focus attention and, at the same time, inhibit casual scanning. Symmetry in social institutions, buildings or symbols is invariably an expression of formal order and centralization; it is heavily geometric. On the other hand, organic symmetry in nature, exemplified by the monarch butterfly, mineral crystals, or the venation of a maple leaf, inspires a sense of wonder and transcendental beauty.

Configuration

Texture

Rough and *smooth* are the basic polarities of texture. Although they are relative, rough usually dominates smooth. This is primarily because rough, dense or complex textures carry more information—there is more to touch, hear and see; and since sensory stimulation is higher, we become more involved—physically and emotionally. Our attention seems focused. On the other hand, smooth surfaces carry less information and are less stimulating to the senses. They promote an attitude of "cool" detachment and passivity; they encourage scanning.

This may help to explain why the smooth surfaces produced by airbrush often seem cold and clinical to painters accustomed to the feel of animal-hair brushes. They miss the stimulation and involvement. It is the same with grounds, that is, painting surfaces. Everyone likes the touch of velvet, but few artists would dare paint on it; the combination of smooth and soft lulls the senses, dissipating any possible expressive power. Linen canvas is vastly preferable—it has just enough grain and grit to elicit emotion from both painter and viewer.

In the art world, the name Van Gogh is practically synonymous with emotion. He developed an impasto technique of painting that resulted in thick, heavily textured surfaces. Not by chance, he combined rough texture with vibrant color for maximum emotional impact.

In music, both blues and rock and roll are usually rough in texture, particularly the vocals. This enhances the expressive power of the music, generating the high audience involvement, sensory and emotional, that is essential to these genres. In this context, the moans, groans, growls and screams of blues balladeers like Muddy Waters and B. B. King or rock stars like Mick Jagger are elements of vocal texture. On the other hand, it is not surprising that teenagers, for whom total, tribal involvement is a must, generally frown on "smooth" music as a symbol of the dull, detached world of adults.

Light and Texture

Smooth surfaces reflect light; rough ones absorb it. The smoother the surface, the more light it reflects. The very smoothest surfaces—highly polished metals, gems or lenses—are highly reflective, sometimes dazzling the eye. Consequently, they easily attract attention and assume dominance.

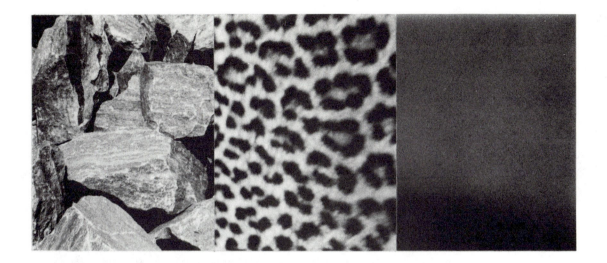

Vincent van Gogh
La Berceuse
Oil on canvas. 36½ × 28½ in.
Bequest of John T. Spaulding
Courtesy, Museum of Fine Arts, Boston

Textural configurations on earth and in outer space show remarkable similarities.   Courtesy of NASA

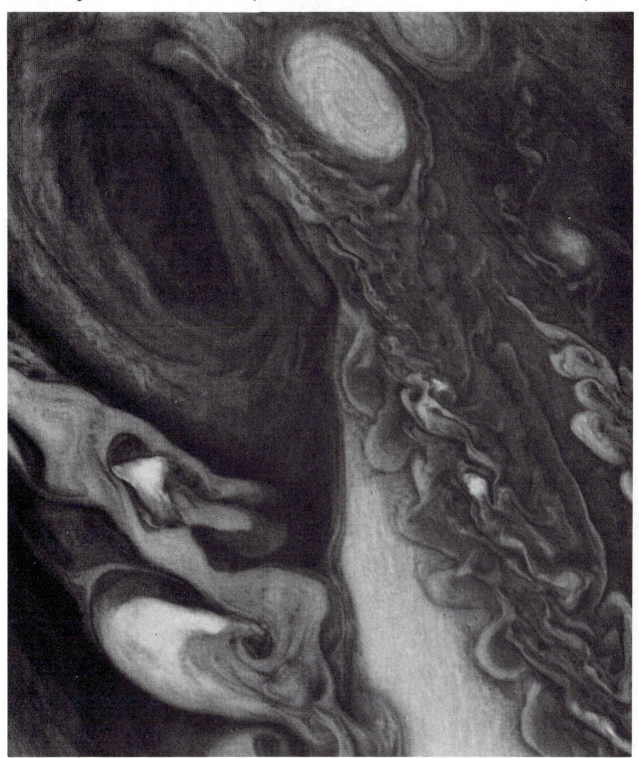

Dissi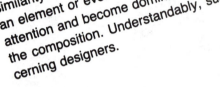ilarity

In design, the element that "is not like the others" tends to get more attention and is often dominant. A circle stands out among squares, a soprano among tenors, a hawk among doves. In a gallery filled with rectangular paintings, an oval one is likely to get the most attention. As a dominance factor, dissimilarity is closely related to both differentiation and contrast. Sometimes an element or event apparently lacking in dominance qualities will gain our attention and become dominant simply because it is unlike anything else in the composition. Understandably, such elements are often deleted by discerning designers.

Frequency

Frequency of Occurrence

Frequency of occurrence generally determines the amount of attention an event will receive. Infrequent or uncommon events often get more attention and become dominant. This also applies to quantities of things. In a painting which contains mostly blue and only a little red, it is the red that stands out and assumes dominance; in a primarily black painting, white is dominant. (For further discussion of frequency, see Part VI, Dynamics.)

The more we see of an event, the less of an event it becomes. Events which occur rarely, like the eruption of a volcano or the election of a president, have status and significance. They are highly visible and dominate our attention. However, frequently occurring events gradually lose their attention-getting power, until, at "critical fusion frequency," they are transformed into fields. They become undifferentiated, blending into an equivalent of the continuous gray tone observed in the revolving disk experiment. See Part VI, Dynamics.

Frequency and Fields

The sun rises and sets every day; a jogger completes her daily mile; birthdays come and go. Events that occur frequently or regularly naturally create rhythms. Some rhythms, like those mentioned above, are easily perceived; others are not. Halley's Comet returns to earth every 76 years, an interval of time much too long to be perceived as a rhythm by the average person. However, in relation to the life span of the earth, a 76-year interval is rather a staccato pulse—an up-tempo rhythm, if you will.

Frequently occurring events create rhythms. The higher the frequency, the more perceptible the rhythm. Try speeding up the sound of normal speech on a tape recorder—after a few minutes you will begin to notice the basic rhythms and inflection patterns (melody) of spoken language. On the other hand, slow down the tape recorder and you will find that rhythm and pattern disappear. Speeding-up enhances pattern recognition (scanning); slowing-down enhances differentiation (focusing). But the relation between frequency and rhythm is important for still another reason—frequently occurring events are not perceived singly or separately, but as part of an encompassing temporal system—a field. Rhythm and pattern are field-oriented systems of organization.

When we speak of rhythm in painting or architecture, we mean implied, rather than actual, rhythm. Rhythm fixed or frozen in space is perceived as pattern; thus when we look at a trail of footprints on a sandy beach or the line of arches in a Roman aqueduct, we sense a rhythm but actually see a pattern. In summary, frequently or regularly occurring events create rhythms if they occur in time and patterns if they occur in space.

QUANTITY AND QUALITY

*"The **more** we see it, the less we **see** it!"*

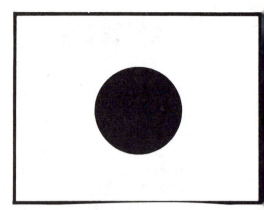

Frequency of occurrence refers to the natural dynamic relationship between quantity and quality. The more something occurs, the less value it has and the less attention it receives. In this context, as frequency increases, significance decreases. This is a well-established principle of economics, commonly expressed as "supply and demand," and a basic tenet of computer logic as well. More importantly, it provides us with a means of addressing the dynamism of art, revealing a continuum in which "quality" is systematically shaped by "quantity."

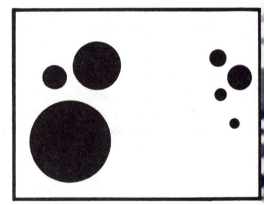

What is the nature of this quality–quantity continuum? Perhaps an analogy will be helpful in answering this question. According to the frequency-of-occurrence principle, the letter "A" has relatively less value than the letter "X" because it appears so much more often. It gets less attention and tends to be taken for granted. By comparison, "X" has high status and is likely to be noticed at once. The relative value, or quality, of "X" and "A" is determined by their frequency of occurrence, or quantity. This suggests a continuum in which all the letters of the alphabet could hypothetically be assigned a value according to their individual frequencies, with "X" and "A" as the polarities. Moreover, the continuum shows that we are equally dependent on both; "X" may be the gold of our alphabet, but "A" is the iron and steel. Frequently occurring letters reveal the texture and sound of our language. Similarly, clichés—frequently occurring ideas and images—reveal the quality and texture of our social fabric.

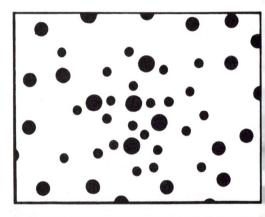

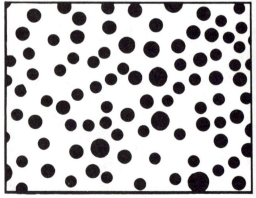

"Art"

"Art" should really be spelled "XRT," for, like the letter "X", it is exceptional, valuable and rare. It requires and gets attention. It behaves exactly like an event, and properly so, for art is an event. It dominates its field—culture—standing in polar juxtaposition to the commonplace and the frequently occurring, that is, clichés, stereotypes, placid assumptions, stock images, ready answers, hack techniques, cheap imitations and conventions of all kinds. Art is an event; its mission is awareness in the mesmerizing field of culture.

In *The Senses,* Otto Lowenstein explains that "as a rule, there is no such thing as a quality code." The intensity of a stimulus is determined by the frequency of the sensory nerve signal. Astonishingly, all of the varied stimuli relayed through our senses are transmitted quantitatively, in terms of impulse frequencies. The translation of frequency into feeling (quantity into quality) begins primarily in the brain, where it is interpolated and gains meaning. This meaning is often modified by subjective factors such as previous experience, sensory bias, cultural norms and even language.

FEELING

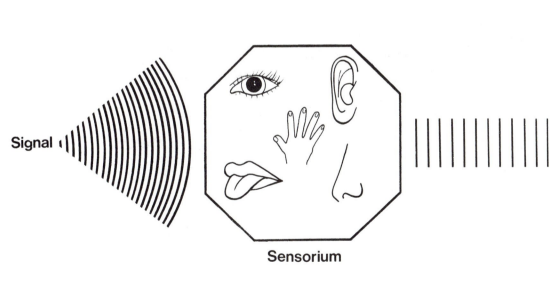

Signal

Sensorium

Modification

Egon Schiele
Mother and Child
Watercolor, black crayon, gouache. 19 × 12½ in.
Courtesy, Museum of Fine Arts, Boston

Cathexis

Cathexis is the degree of psychological or emotional energy associated with an element or event. An event with a high degree of cathexis normally gets a lot of attention and assumes dominance. In visual art, the psychological-emotional impact of the human face cannot be overestimated. It is highly charged with cathexis and immediately attracts the viewer's eye. A face in the wrong place spells disaster in design. Hollywood exploits sex and violence for their obvious attention-getting ability; third-rate newspapers sell themselves on the shock value of their headlines. Status symbols, such as luxury cars, and national symbols, like flags and anthems, both utilize cathexis in the same way. Cathexis is equally important in subjective content and objective form. Contemporary anthropology teaches that every culture has a unique "program" with its own customs, biases, assumptions, perceptions and values. Each culture also has its own catalogue for cathexis; what is highly charged with emotion in one culture is often bland in another.

In *Language, Thought, and Reality,* Benjamin Whorf explores the coding of cathexis in language and how it varies from culture to culture. He explains that each mother-tongue molds its own idea of meaning and, ultimately, reality. Whorf writes, "And every language is a vast pattern-system, different from others, in which are culturally ordained the forms and categories by which the personality not only communicates, but also analyzes nature, notices or neglects types of relationship and phenomena, channels his reasoning, and builds the house of his consciousness." He explains that "language is the great symbolism from which other symbolisms take their cue." In the animal world, smells and sounds are heavily laden with cathexis. A zoologist tells of how a young hyena he was transporting in a vehicle ignored lions he could see but couldn't smell, but upon smelling them instantly panicked. Many territorial animals are known to mark the limits of their territory by urinating, thereby warning would-be trespassers away. This suggests an olfactory conception of space which is quite foreign to us as visually oriented beings. In music, the astute composer understands the cathexis associated with different sounds apart from their role in a melody or arrangement. Igor Stravinsky was a master of evocative sound; his work *The Rite of Spring* brilliantly demonstrates the importance of cathexis in sound and music.

Just as Stravinsky's music is based on the psychic and emotional import of sound, many poets have been similarly concerned with the sound of words in poetry. They have investigated the cathexis of spoken language as abstract sound, apart from literal meaning. The French Symbolist poet Arthur Rimbaud is typical. He even explored the relationship between sound and color, assigning a different hue to each vowel. His poems often contain seemingly illogical images—names of places, unearthly terrain and strange color associations. The effect is one of psychic resonance in which word-meaning is subordinate to feeling—cathexis.

"Vowels"

A black, E white, I red, U green, O blue: vowels,
One day I will tell your latent birth:
A, black hairy corset of shining flies
which buzz around cruel stench,
Gulfs of darkness; E, whiteness of vapors and tents,
Lances of proud glaciers, white kings, quivering of flowers;
I, purples, spit blood, laughter of beautiful lips
In anger or penitent drunkeness;

U, cycles, divine vibrations of green seas,
Peace of pastures scattered with animals, peace of the wrinkles
Which alchemy prints on heavy studious brows;

O, supreme Clarion full of strange stridor,
Silences crossed by worlds and angels:
—O, the Omega, violet beam from his eyes!

Arthur Rimbaud

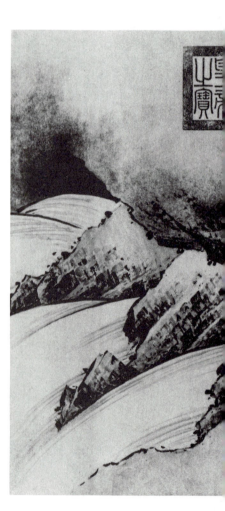

Synesthesia, the translation of information from one sense into another, is a widely practiced technique of poets but is by no means limited to poetry. Many painters use similar means in their medium. James Whistler's titles often suggest synesthesia: *Nocturne in Black and Gold* and *Symphony in White.* Mondrian's *Broadway Boogie Woogie* and Picasso's *The Three Musicians* are similar attempts at sensory cross reference.

Symbols with so-called universal authority are sometimes called *archetypes.* Carl Jung, an imaginative and broadly educated psychologist, explored the concept of archetypal symbols rooted in a collective unconscious shared by all human beings. He focused particular attention on the role of art in visualizing and perpetuating such symbols for the benefit of culture, often looking to primitive and tribal art for verification of his theories. The famed Austrian "Venus of Willendorf" is a prehistoric stone figurine with full, rounded forms suggestive of female fertility. As a symbol, it conveys today roughly the same message that it did 15,000 years ago; thus it may be considered an archetype. However, such assumptions are not without risk; the actual meaning and value of the "Venus" is inextricably tied to the environment which produced it—it belongs to another world.

Ch'en Jung
The Nine Dragon Scroll (detail)
Francis Gardner Curtis Fund
Courtesy, Museum of Fine Arts, Boston

At the height of the "Woodstock" era, Jimi Hendrix used both synesthesia and cathexis to create musical experiences of tremendous vitality and emotion. His unique, imaginative adaptation of the guitar to the high-powered world of electric technology stunned audiences and inspired musicians. The electric guitar became a cultural symbol of almost mythic dimensions, somehow embodying both mystic past and technological future. The cult of the guitar persists even today, its cathexis widely known and exploited.

Cathexis is the central feature of all symbols. Understandably, the most powerful symbols carry the most cathexis; the holy cross or crucifix, the American flag, a full moon, mandala or swastika, a human skull, lions, eagles, swords, stars, rockets, arrows, rainbows, eyes, infants, pyramids and tombstones, weathered old men and voluptuous young women. There is a great deal of literature on symbology, for wherever there is culture there are symbols. In fact, much of what we know about vanished civilizations comes to us through their surviving symbology invested in their art, architecture or domestic crafts, recovered and restored by archaeologists.

Mycerinus and Queen
From Giza, Dynasty IV (2599-2571 B.C.)
Harvard Boston Expedition
Courtesy, Museum of Fine Arts, Boston
Harvard Boston Expedition

Philip Paratore
Venus of Weymouth
Pencil. 18 × 24 in.

Anthony Panzera
Self-Portrait
Pencil

168

Cathexis

The attention-getting power and cathexis of the human face can scarcely be overestimated; it naturally focuses attention and stimulates emotion.

(*below*) Kathë Kollwitz
The Mothers
Drawing, India ink and Chinese white. 18 × 23½ in.
Allen Collection
Courtesy, Museum of Fine Arts, Boston

(*opposite page, top*) Kunimasa
Nakamura Nakago as Matsuo-Maru in Suzawara Denju Tenarai Kagami
Woodblock print
Courtesy, Museum of Fine Arts, Boston

(*opposite page, bottom*) Large censor—Maya style
Courtesy of the American Museum of Natural History, New York

Cathexis

In the modern world of mass production and consumption, slick ads, catchy slogans and computer-crafted sales pitches, symbols are born and buried every day. Mass media enfeebles cultural symbolism through overexposure and repetition (high frequency-of-occurrence); it makes clichés of everything. Even the most poignant symbols seem faded in the crush of press- and video-spawned images. As a result, the historic function of symbols, and art itself, has become dubious and is questioned by artists concerned with the vitality of their statements. Many have abandoned symbolism as an effective way to communicate ideas, and, like conceptual artists, rely heavily on process in an attempt to regain the initiative in art. However, an understanding of cathexis is essential in all forms of art and communication. It is a dominance factor of major importance.

Content

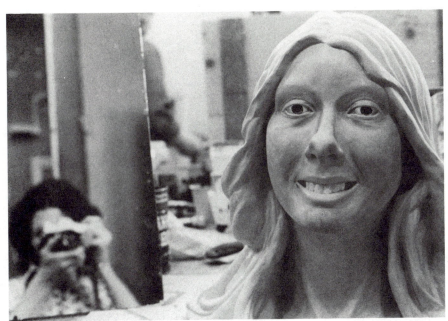

Rana Patterson
Self-Portrait
Clay

Content refers to subject or subject matter. It is what the book, painting, movie or poem is about. Content is the message. It is the story in literature and the melody in music; it is the plot, the theme and the motif. Content naturally monopolizes our attention and so, broadly speaking, it may be considered a dominance factor.

Content usually involves recognizable things: people, places, objects, events or situations. Cézanne's apples and Renoir's women are typical artistic subjects; so are seagulls, barns, sailboats, autumn trees and sunsets. What makes a Cézanne still life different from one in a tourist gallery is his concern for structure and form, which paved the way for abstraction in the twentieth century. Modern sculptors and painters eventually deleted content from their works, espousing an aesthetic of pure form. Similarly, modern composers such as Stravinsky and Schoenberg explored the concept of music without melody.

We habitually look for content in art. When confronted with unfamiliar or abstract imagery, we seek a recognizable element, something to which we can relate. Such elements become the focus of attention and easily assume dominance. On the other hand, in content-oriented images containing an abundance of recognizable elements or events, cathexis becomes a key factor in determining dominance.

The relationship between content and form is polar and juxtapositional. In general, as the value of content increases, the value of form decreases. And conversely, as the value of content decreases, that of form increases.

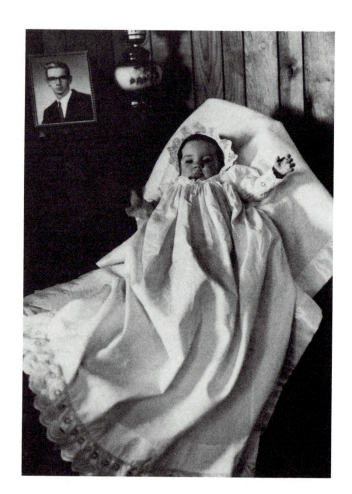

and Form

Paul Cézanne
Fruit and Jug
Oil on canvas. 12¾ × 16 in.
Bequest of John T. Spaulding
Courtesy, Museum of Fine Arts, Boston

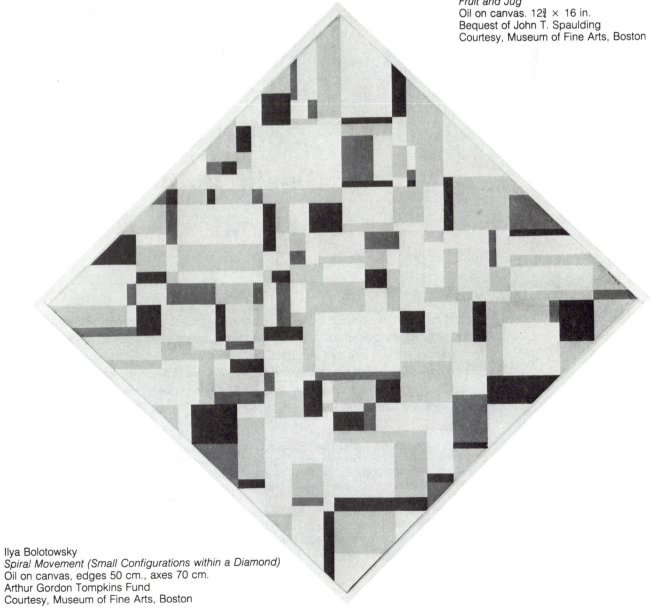

Ilya Bolotowsky
Spiral Movement (Small Configurations within a Diamond)
Oil on canvas, edges 50 cm., axes 70 cm.
Arthur Gordon Tompkins Fund
Courtesy, Museum of Fine Arts, Boston

Confluence of Dominance Factors

In design, as in nature, dominance is usually established by a combination or confluence of dominance factors. Only rarely does one factor alone account for dominance. When a group of factors is working together, the result is stronger structure and better design. On the other hand, poorly organized dominance factors will often compete, clash or cancel each other, resulting in confusion.

In "El Jaleo" we can identify at least seven major dominance factors:

Light

Contrast

Cathexis

Movement

Definition

Dissimilarity

Number

Absolute Dominance?

Just as there is no such thing as absolute quiet, at least on earth, neither is there absolute dominance. Every dominant event is relative to its field and to the disposition of other events. Dominance factors freely interact, combine and converge, revealing a system capable of great flexibility and change. As our understanding of such organic systems improves, absolutism appears increasingly irrelevant.

Seven dominance factors in "El Jaleo" (opposite page) are: (1) light—on dancer (primary event); (2) contrast—dark against light (primary relationship); (3) cathexis—in dancer's dramatic gesture; (4) movement—dancer's informal, spontaneous motion set in counterpoint to the formal row of seated musicians and spectators (note reference to position in the two guitars hanging on the wall); (5) definition—well-defined head, arms and dress of dancer are heightened by soft-edged, shadowy middle ground; (6) dissimilarity—the dancer is the only standing figure in the foreground; (7) number—expressed in the dominance of the one outstanding event, "El Jaleo"—the dancer.

John Singer Sargent
El Jaleo
Oil on canvas
Isabella Stewart Gardner Museum, Boston

PART IV
APPLICATIONS

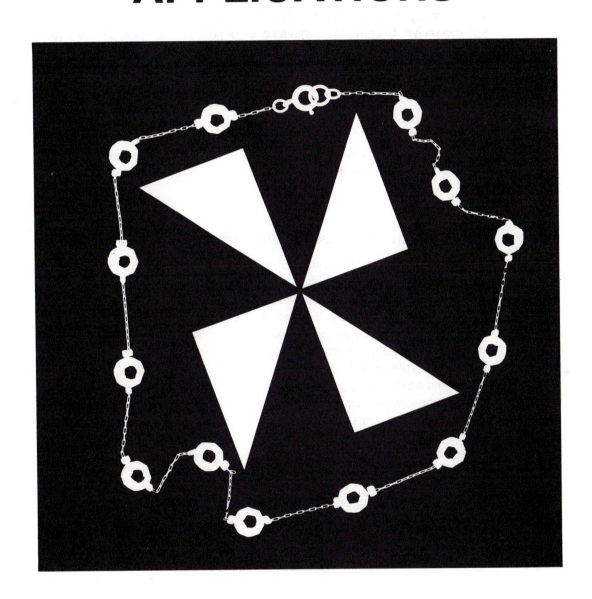

In Part V, Major Matrices, we will provide an inventory of polar adjectives, the building blocks of a theoretical language of design. However, in the abstract form of an inventory, this language may appear somewhat foreign to the reader. And so it might be helpful first to briefly describe the system and explore its application to a working situation—the studio or classroom.

The inventory is divided into four matrices: conceptual, structural, dynamic, and evaluative. Each matrix contains a list of polar terms which can be used to discuss and analyze design. Previously, pages 28 through 30 (Practicum) showed how polar terms such as light and dark can be used in a question and answer format to objectively describe a painting. The following paragraphs include exercises which will further develop the student's ability to understand and discuss design.

The four matrices comprise an organized whole. However, to facilitate discussion, they are presented here as a four-stage sequence.

Stage One: The Conceptual Matrix

In this stage, the task is to establish a basic conceptual vocabulary that will lend meaning and direction to the exercises that follow in stage two. This involves the definition and description of the polar adjectives listed in the conceptual matrix inventory. It is important that these definitions be objective and specific, but that their application be speculative and general. For example, the concept of "harmony" should be defined as precisely as possible and then explored in a wide variety of applications: painting, poetry, photojournalism, architecture, philosophy and so on. Often, such concepts can be nicely demonstrated within the context of daily living: dress codes, home decoration, social interaction, vernacular, cultural traditions and institutions. Establishing a basic conceptual matrix is an essential first step; its development and refinement is an ongoing, life-long learning experience.

A useful exercise would be to create a visual catalogue of key terms in the conceptual matrix. This would typically include:

Field—Event
Harmony—Contrast
Organic—Geometric
General—Specific
Simple—Complex
Formal—Informal

(The medium varies with the emphasis of the studio or course, *i.e.*, watercolor, gouache, pencil, pastel, clay, wood, etc.)

Stage Two: The Structural Matrix

In the second stage of our design experience we look closely at the mediums and materials we are about to use. We explore their physical characteristics and make a visual or verbal inventory of their capabilities and effects. In short, we try to find out what the medium can do. An introductory exploration of oil painting, for example, might involve a series of exercises based on the following polar relationships:

Thick—Thin
Warm—Cool
Light—Dark
Opaque—Transparent
Bright—Dull

An exploration of clay might involve a similar series of exercises:

Rough—Smooth
Thick—Thin
Large—Small
Wet—Dry
Solid—Hollow

Exercises exploring a nonvisual medium, such as speech or sound, might include:

Quiet—Loud
Soft—Hard
Long—Short
Clear—Vague
Slow—Fast

Small-scale demonstration pieces in which particular physical characteristics are isolated and studied are extremely helpful. They reveal the grammar of the language of design. Our primary purpose is to learn about the medium with which we are working, but it is not unusual for major ideas to evolve from such exercises. Indeed, much of modern painting seems to have had the same goal—the exploration of paint itself. On a loftier, more philosophical level, Marshall McLuhan expressed a similar notion when he coined the phrase "The medium is the message."

Stage Three: The Dynamic Matrix

In stage three, materials and mediums are objectively studied to determine their functional characteristics, listed under "Energy" and "Condition" in the inventory. Again, the purpose is understanding through experience. A series of small-scale studies and exercises, each one focusing on a specific pair of polar adjectives in the dynamic matrix and applied to a particular medium, provides a personal reference of lasting utility. These exercises seem to be most beneficial if they are purely abstract and not tied to any subject matter. In this way, the functional characteristics of the medium may be more freely explored and directly experienced. In general, understanding one's medium is a prelude to the expression of ideas.

A series of exercises exploring illustration or drawing might involve the following typical polar relationships:

Positive—Negative
Planned—Spontaneous
Complete—Incomplete
Fast—Slow
Graceful—Awkward

Stage Four: The Evaluative Matrix

In this stage, the emphasis is on the development of verbal and analytical skills. The terms listed in the evaluative matrix are defined and their application to a wide range of mediums and disciplines discussed. Both art history and art criticism may be easily integrated at this point, often resulting in an increased sense of relevance all around. The goal is an ideal marriage of sensitive perception and accurate description.

Definitions, in art, are often more meaningful if they are accompanied by visual examples. For this reason, a series of exercises cataloguing key terms in the evaluative matrix inventory, with visual examples from art history, commercial art and one's own sketchbook, is extremely valuable.

Typical terms in this visual catalogue would be:

Classical—Romantic
Objective—Subjective
Emotional—Intellectual
Decorative—Evocative
Abstract—Narrative

The cataloguing exercises are an important first step towards understanding the basic polar dynamics of design. They are particularly helpful in developing an effective common vocabulary, without which discussions of art often become hopelessly vague and subjective. It is also important to regularly review and discuss a wide variety of works of art to further develop critical abilities. The matrices should be an integral part of these discursive exercises, as shown previously in the "practicum" on page 28. Of course, there are many ways to integrate the matrices into the design dialogue, depending on teaching style, the type of course and so on. The goals of these exercises, however, should be kept clearly in mind: accurate perception, objective description and consistent terminology.

Art may be compared to a language that we must learn to understand and speak. To continue the analogy, we could say that design is the infrastructure of that language. In order to learn to speak any language fluently, at least three things are necessary: (1) a consistent, common vocabulary; (2) a grammar or set of organizational principles; and (3) practical experience. Field-event theory provides the grammar, the matrices provide the common vocabulary, and the exercises just described provide the practical experience. All this, however, is only the beginning—a foundation. For eloquence in any language, especially the language of art, requires long-term personal involvement and commitment. The work is arduous, but joyous. The rewards are great.

In Part IV, Applications, our purpose has been to show how the major matrices can be used to study design in the workshop, classroom or studio. But our larger purpose has been to encourage the integration of theory and practice, for one tends to languish without the other. Indeed, application is a crucial component of any genuine learning experience.

MAJOR MATRICES

PART V

Major Matrices

An Inventory

Field-event relationships are formed by two differing sets of characteristics or properties, generally expressed in terms of polar adjectives such as "simple–complex," "soft–hard" or "light–dark." These sets are the essential building blocks of all relationships, the alphabet in the language of design.

The next few pages contain an inventory of these graphic characteristics, presented as sets of polar adjectives. It is extensive and comprehensive, relevant to both visual and nonvisual design. For clarity and ease of handling, it has been divided into four major matrices:

       I.   **CONCEPTUAL**

      II.   **STRUCTURAL**

          A. *Primary Physical Characteristics*

          B. *Secondary Physical Characteristics*

     III.   **DYNAMIC**

          A. *Energy*

          B. *Condition*

     IV.   **EVALUATIVE**

These matrices are closely related to what Philip Osgood called "factors" in his book, *The Measurement of Meaning*. They provide the basis for a semantic analysis of design.

Conceptual Matrix

Field - - - - - Event

Harmony - - - - - Contrast

Simple - - - - - Complex

Organic - - - - - Geometric

Informal - - - - - Formal

Low-Definition - - - - - High-Definition

General - - - - - Specific

Uniformity - - - - - Variety

Dynamic - - - - - Static

Form - - - - - Content

Subjective - - - - - Objective

Intuitive - - - - - Rational

Emotional - - - - - Intellectual

Evocative - - - - - Decorative

Narrative - - - - - Abstract

Structural Matrix

A. *Primary Physical Characteristics*

Light - - - - - Dark

Large - - - - - Small

Angular - - - - - Circular

Warm - - - - - Cool

Deep - - - - - Shallow

Opaque - - - - - Transparent

Slow - - - - - Fast

Close - - - - - Far

Flat - - - - - Dimensional

Hard-edged - - - - - Soft-edged

Soft - - - - - Hard

Quiet - - - - - Loud

Blunt - - - - - Sharp

Rough - - - - - Smooth

Clear - - - - - Vague

Thick - - - - - Thin

B. *Secondary Physical Characteristics*

Wide - - - - - Narrow	Saturated - - - - - Diluted
Wet - - - - - Dry	Crude - - - - - Slick
Glossy - - - - - Matte	Fat - - - - - Thin
Clean - - - - - Dirty	Slippery - - - - - Sticky
Neat - - - - - Sloppy	Sweet - - - - - Sour
Coarse - - - - - Fine	Light - - - - - Heavy
Strong - - - - - Weak	Opened - - - - - Closed
Bold - - - - - Meek	Dense - - - - - Sparse
Graceful - - - - - Awkward	Full - - - - - Empty
Long - - - - - Short	Lush - - - - - Bare
Solid - - - - - Hollow	Rich - - - - - Poor
Convex - - - - - Concave	Framed - - - - - Unframed
Delicate - - - - - Massive	Old - - - - - Young
Miniature - - - - - Monumental	Healthy - - - - - Sick
Ornate - - - - - Plain	Intense - - - - - Lax
Focused - - - - - Unfocused	Horizontal - - - - - Vertical

Dynamic Matrix

A. *Energy*

Passive - - - - - Active

Advance - - - - - Recede

Attack - - - - - Decay

Periodic - - - - - Erratic

Tension - - - - - Relaxation

Contraction - - - - - Expansion

Attraction - - - - - Repulsion

Absorption - - - - - Reflection

Serial - - - - - Simultaneous

Direct - - - - - Circuitous

Convergent - - - - - Divergent

Steady - - - - - Fluctuating

Internal - - - - - External

Agitation - - - - - Tranquility

Movement - - - - - Fixity

Explosion - - - - - Implosion

B. *Condition*

Symmetrical - - - - - Asymmetrical	Positive - - - - - Negative
Balance - - - - - Imbalance	Planned - - - - - Spontaneous
Measurable - - - - - Immeasurable	Complete - - - - - Incomplete
Regular - - - - - Irregular	Ordered - - - - - Random
Predictable - - - - - Unpredictable	Integration - - - - - Segregation
Intrinsic - - - - - Extrinsic	Detachment - - - - - Involvement
Lucid - - - - - Obscure	Concord - - - - - Discord
Enclosed - - - - - Open	Consolidation - - - - - Dispersion
Flexible - - - - - Rigid	Centralization - - - - - Decentralization
Figure - - - - - Ground	Gradual - - - - - Abrupt
Singularity - - - - - Multiplicity	Constant - - - - - Intermittent
Minimum - - - - - Maximum	Chromatic - - - - - Achromatic
Permanent - - - - - Temporary	Tonal - - - - - Atonal

Evaluative Matrix

Romantic - - - - - Classical

Subjective - - - - - Objective

Emotional - - - - - Intellectual

Abstract - - - - - Narrative

Original - - - - - Imitation

Innovative - - - - - Conventional

Good - - - - - Bad

Meaningful - - - - - Meaningless

Natural - - - - - Artificial

Beautiful - - - - - Ugly

Sophisticated - - - - - Naive

Cliché - - - - - Visionary

Ordinary - - - - - Extraordinary

Challenging - - - - - Boring

Decorative - - - - - Evocative

Consonant - - - - - Dissonant

Peaceful - - - - - Aggressive

Pleasurable - - - - - Painful

Stimulating - - - - - Monotonous

Stylish - - - - - Primitive

Modern - - - - - Old-fashioned

Flamboyant - - - - - Restrained

Progressive - - - - - Conservative

Masculine - - - - - Feminine

Difficult - - - - - Easy

Summary

A summary of our design model shows that:

1. **Fields and field-event relationships are the primary organizational systems in design; they represent two poles of a continuum.**

2. **Fields are formed by uniform sets of characteristics or properties.**

3. **Field-event relationships are formed by differing sets of characteristics or properties.**

4. **The key differentiating agent in all relationships is contrast. High-, medium- and low-contrast signify degrees of differentiation.**

5. **Relationships in design are subdivided into three general groups: primary, secondary and peripheral relationships.**

6. **Relationships are generally hierarchical in structure; they are dominance-oriented systems of organization.**

7. **The characteristics or properties of which relationships consist are presented as sets of polar adjectives.**

8. **In a set of polar adjectives, one of the polarities tends to be dominant.**

9. **An inventory of polar adjectives is organized into four major matrices.**

10. **The major matrices provide a basis for a semantic analysis of design.**

DYNAMICS

PART VI

An elegant experiment with a revolving disk, painted half black and half white, demonstrates an important principle of perception. Revolving on its axis, the speed, or frequency, of the disk is gradually increased. As the disk spins faster and faster, it becomes increasingly difficult to distinguish between the white and black side of the disk. The viewer begins to experience some sensory stress. As the disk's speed continues to increase, a flicker is visible in which black and white pulse intermittently. At flicker frequency, eye discomfort and fatigue become maximum. It would seem that any further increase in speed would be pure sensory torture, but, to our relief, it is not. As speed is again increased, flickering ceases, and the black and white sides of the disk fuse into continuous gray. This is called *critical fusion frequency*.

Critical Fusion

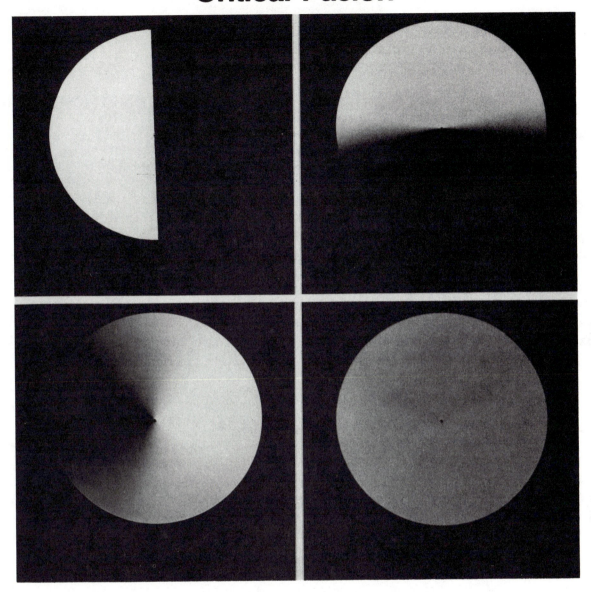

The disk experiment is significant in several ways. First, it underlines the relationship between differentiation and acuity in vision. When the disk is still or slow-moving, differentiation is maximum and so is visual acuity. In the middle, flicker range, differentiation is low and acuity is vastly diminished. This loss of acuity is accompanied by sensory discomfort and stress. At critical fusion frequency, there is *no* differentiation and normal visual acuity is restored.

In *Light and Vision,* Conrad Mueller explains that "intermittent stimulation appears to be another factor crucial to acuity . . . acuity being best when the frequency of flashes is either so low that each flash can be seen individually, or so high that fusion occurs. In the middle range, where flicker is visible, acuity is at its worst." Because of its apparently heavy impact on sensory perception, critical fusion is of great significance to designers and all those interested in effective communication.

Critical fusion is well-dramatized by the revolving disk, but this phenomenon is by no means limited to objects in motion. Static visual material shares the same overall pattern, as some simple analogical conjecture may help to demonstrate.

Critical Density

The concept of critical fusion frequency translates easily into still or static visual material by substituting the word "density" for "frequency." The spinning disk is measured in time as cycles per second, or frequency. Static visual material is measured in space as units per area, or density. We determine critical fusion density in much the same way that we determine critical fusion frequency. Furthermore, the sensory pattern is essentially the same.

The printed page is a typical piece of static visual information. As the quantity of print on a page increases, differentiation decreases, and acuity correspondingly decreases. On most book pages the density of print falls into the middle, flicker range, well short of critical fusion. Interestingly, this is the discomfort and stress zone of sensory perception. One can't help but wonder at the sly irony of it all. The printed book, symbol of literacy and Western civilization, guarantees discomfort and fatigue to all by its very form.

Critical fusion density is not a novel notion. The dot patterns used in halftone reproduction are based on the same idea. These dot patterns can easily be seen on any newspaper photo with the help of a small magnifying glass. However, not all dot patterns are the same; some screens contain more dots than others. They have a greater dot density and are capable of more faithful reproduction. But all halftone screens work essentially the same way—the image is formed at the point of critical fusion density.

The exploration of critical fusion in painting is best illustrated by Impressionism. Impressionist painters, such as Monet, Pissaro and Seurat, interpreted subject matter as fields of light which could be broken down into discrete "light-values." They then used individual flecks, dots or "points" of paint to reconstruct these light-values on canvas. From the correct viewing distance, one is not aware of the individual dots or flecks of pigment, for they are calculated to fuse in the eye of the viewer in what is sometimes called a "visual mix." Seurat's development of Pointillism seems to have been modestly prophetic in its anticipation of dot-pattern technology, so commonplace in commercial reproduction today.

Video uses critical fusion in much the same way as Impressionistic painting or halftone reproduction. The video image is broken down into discrete light-values, called "picture elements," which are uniformly distributed on a grid. Each individual element receives an electric signal, the strength of which determines the value of the light at that point, or "light-value." A close-up look at the image formed on your television's picture screen will show it to be quite immaterial and "abstract," consisting of pulsing patterns of constantly changing points of light. Just as in Pointillist painting, the image "comes together," that is, coheres, in the eye of the viewer at the correct viewing distance. In both television and Impressionism, an understanding of critical fusion seems to be essential.

The synthesizer can be used to demonstrate critical fusion in the auditory sense. The synthesizer's primary sound generator is the oscillator. All oscillators have a frequency range, and every frequency corresponds to a tone. If, starting at zero, we gradually increase the frequency of the oscillator, a tone is emitted in the shape of a staccato pulse. As the frequency is increased further, the pitch of the tone rises and its tempo increases, eventually reaching the audio equivalent of flicker frequency. At this frequency, our ears experience discomfort and stress, just as our eyes did with the spinning disk. Soon after, the accelerating staccato pulse is fused into a continuous tone, informing us that we have reached critical fusion frequency.

Students of cinema are familiar with a principle known as persistence of vision, which refers to the illusion of continuity in films. The image seen on the screen is actually formed by separate film frames, discrete, still photographs which are projected at a frequency measured in frames per second, calculated to achieve critical fusion. This fusion takes place in the eye of the viewer, as does the fusion of dots in a newsphoto, reminding us once again that we are dealing with a vital pattern of sensory perception, relevant to a broad range of mediums. Moreover, this pattern is not limited to vision; it also applies to our auditory and kinetic senses and may well prove to be applicable to our entire sensorium.

Critical Fusion

Critical fusion works the same way in traditional forms of music. Instruments such as the guitar, piano or saxophone are played rhythmically, with a beat or tempo. As the tempo of the music increases, it goes through the same pattern of changes described in the spinning disk experiment. At slow tempos, contrast and differentiation are high; at moderate tempos, they are low. And at fast tempos—flicker frequency—differentiation may become painfully difficult or impossible, profoundly affecting both performers and audience.

Jazz is an idiom that often explores speed in music; the popular connotation of *jazzy* is "up-beat" and "up-tempo." In the 1970s, John McLaughlin dazzled audiences with his high-speed electric guitar playing. His jazz-rock band, the Mahavishnu Orchestra, based its early successes on its overwhelming high speed and precision. But it was not to last. Ironically, "fusion jazz," as it came to be known, rarely reached critical fusion. It more often remained at flicker frequency, the sensory stress range preceding critical fusion. Understandably, such performance styles eventually exhaust even the most devoted of audiences.

Critical fusion is a crucial component of field-event theory. Not only does it affect our sensorium, but also our approach to the structure and organization of information in general. As such, it bears directly on our model of design.

Metamorphosis

We have postulated a design continuum with two polarities: (1) fields and (2) field-event relationships. We have also described a metamorphosis in which decreasing differentiation and contrast leads a field-event relationship to become a field. The point at which this occurs is critical fusion. When such a metamorphosis takes place in time, the correct term is critical fusion *frequency;* in space, it is critical fusion *density.*

The harmony–contrast continuum illustrates an identical metamorphosis. When contrast falls below a certain point, known as a threshold, it loses its power of differentiation and becomes *harmony.* This threshold is synonymous with critical fusion.

The diagram above shows a series of rectangles graphically
symbolizing metamorphosis through the increasing density
of events (vertical bars): a solid white field metamorphoses
slowly into a solid black field. Steps 4, 5, and 6 (the "middle
range") display decreasing sensory acuity and increasing
ambiguity.

FIELD-EVENT DYNAMICS

In art that stresses content, contrast is a differentiating agent. Hence, narrative and realistic art tend to be high in contrast. When content is unimportant, literal meaning is correspondingly low; the emphasis is on form. In such cases, contrast may or may not be high, depending on the idea of the design. This indicates that the relationship between contrast and content is rather one-sided; it is possible to have contrast without content, but not content without contrast.

A lone shade tree on a barren plain has high content-value. It is also high in contrast and well differentiated. The same tree in a forest is poorly differentiated and has less value. As the size or density of the forest increases, the value of the tree decreases still further. It is now part of the field and has no content-value; if it were cut down one night, no one would notice.

Quantitative Analysis: A Summary

As the density or frequency of a field increases, differentiation decreases. Conversely, as density or frequency decreases, differentiation increases.

As the density or frequency of a field increases, contrast decreases. Conversely, as density or frequency decreases, contrast increases.

As differentiation decreases, contrast decreases. Conversely, as differentiation increases, contrast increases.

As differentiation decreases, content-value decreases. Conversely, as differentiation increases, the value of content increases.

As the size, density, or frequency of a field increases, differentiation, contrast, and content-value decrease.

A full moon suspended in an evening sky is a field-event relationship of high differentiation, high contrast and high content-value. The same moon at midday is poorly differentiated and has little content-value. The phases of the moon well illustrate the pattern of changes in the "rising and setting" of a field-event relationship.

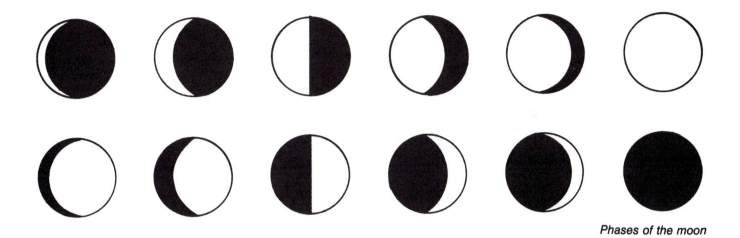

Phases of the moon

The diagram below shows the correlation between density and value; note the decreasing value of single events (dots) as their density increases.

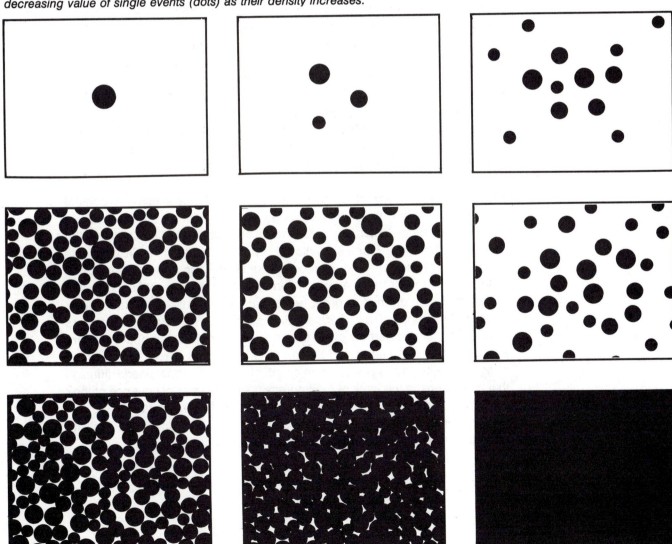

FIELD-EVENT DYNAMICS

The more field-oriented a design is, the lower the value of its content.

The more event-oriented a design is, the higher the value of its content.

Paintings that stress content, like portraits or landscapes, are event-oriented and based on relationships. This is naturally encouraged by the subject matter itself. However, not all paintings with subject matter follow the same pattern. Some painters use subject matter of apparently high content-value to form fields. Richard Estes, superrealist, city-scene painter, is an example. To Estes, buildings, signs, windows and reflections, buses, cars, streetlights, shopkeepers, and pedestrians are all like so many trees in a forest. Ironically, they have little content value in his paintings, for his real interest is in creating fields. In *The Urban Landscape,* Estes explains, "It's a matter of balancing the painting so that all of the parts are of equal interest." With a little daring, this may be interpreted to mean "of equal and uniform value," affirming the field-oriented character of his work.

Expressionism in either art or music is event-oriented. The stress is on content and message rather than form, although the exploration of the expressive properties of form—color, rhythm, texture and, above all, contrast—is the hallmark of the best Expressionistic art. Painters like Munch, Ensor, Nolde and Oskar Kokoschka—and composers like Beethoven and Wagner—often juxtaposed heroic or tragic events (figures) against a turbulent field (society) to create human dramas of great emotional import. Unlike the stark figure-ground statements of the German Expressionists, Impressionistic figures were often blended harmoniously into their grounds. Even so heavy a figure as a cathedral was interpreted by Monet to behave as a field, relinquishing its figure quality and its power as an event. The radiant, atmospheric diffusion that characterized the work of the Impressionists was a consequence of their bias toward unified fields; light was only a vehicle toward that end. After all, in an earlier age, Rembrandt used the same vehicle, light, toward an opposite end—the optimum articulation of field-event relationships.

Claude Monet
Rouen Cathedral: Early Morning, Tour Albane
Oil on canvas. 106 × 74 cm.
Purchase of Arthur Gordon Tompkins Residuary Fund
Courtesy, Museum of Fine Arts, Boston

Simple and Complex Fields

Between macrocosm and microcosm are an inestimable number and variety of fields, far too many to encompass with the imagination. However, we can distinguish between two broad categories: simple and complex fields. Contrast is more readily achieved with simple fields. On a blank, white page or a blanket of new-fallen snow, contrast is easily stated, events easily differentiated. Conversely, contrast and differentiation are difficult to achieve in complex fields.

High-, medium- and low-contrast are general terms, referring to degrees of differentiation. High-contrast relationships, such as black against white or a police siren in the dead of night, yield maximum sensation. Low-contrast relationships are much more subtle and subdued. But when the degree of contrast falls beneath a certain threshold, critical fusion frequency, the event loses its identity and merges with the field. The threshold varies with the complexity of the field.

The simpler the field, the lower the threshold; and conversely, the more complex the field, the higher the threshold.

SIMPLE

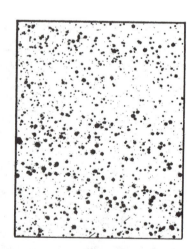

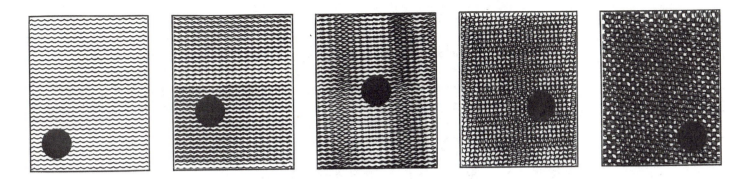

The series of illustrations above shows that an event is more easily established on a simple field than on a complex one; as the complexity of the field increases, the value (attention-getting power) of the event decreases.

COMPLEX

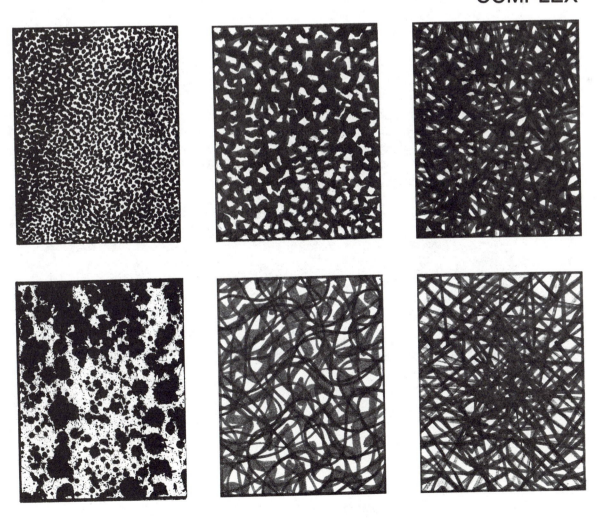

In a Japanese rock garden, there are two main elements: rocks and sand. The sand is raked with painstaking care into uniform patterns and textures, making a simple but eloquent field. Contrast is provided by specially chosen rocks of various sizes and shapes which are carefully arranged on the sand, much like islands in a sea. The juxtaposition between rocks and sand is metaphorical: "The Japanese garden is like a still picture—a frozen moment which is also all eternity." At the seashore, wind and surf create an acoustic field, perfectly pierced by the cries of gulls. The expressive power of simple field-event relationships is apparent. A cloudless sky, a still pond, and a blank canvas are simple fields, but the simplest field is silence. As all dramatists know, silence can make an event out of the slightest cough or rustle. On the other hand, forests are complex fields, tending to obscure rather than heighten events. Nature photographers quickly learn that good exposures are hard to find in dense forests because of the lack of contrast and differentiation; nothing stands out. Cities are much worse. They are bottomless melting pots that absorb and assimilate everything. Cities are roughly equivalent to black holes in outer space. They are fields of enormous density and frequency. In the supercomplex acoustic field of city traffic, nothing less than a fire engine's screaming siren can presume to command the slightest attention. Understandably, it takes an extraordinary event to make an impression on a seasoned New Yorker!

The traditional Japanese house or temple is a wooden-frame structure with a tile roof, oiled paper walls and sliding room dividers. It is spare and simple; decoration is minimal. On the inside, the motif is the rectangle; shapes and spaces are molded after the "tatami" mat—a well-proportioned, rectangular floor mat found in all Japanese interior design. The effect is classical: balance, order, restraint, economy and simplicity. In dramatic contrast, traditional Japanese dress is elaborate and lively. This is well-illustrated by the kimono, garb of the geisha—boldly designed floral patterns or abstract calligraphy; colorful multi-patterns, playful but perfect—a dazzling display for the eye. At first, the apparent disparity between Japanese dress and architecture is baffling; they seem to point to opposite ethnic values. But suddenly, it makes sense: a complex event in a simple field—an ideal field-event relationship.

The reverse seems to be true in Arabic and Islamic countries. Traditional state and religious architecture is extraordinarily lavish in decoration and design. Intricate, mosaic-like patterns often cover the walls, floors and even ceilings, creating three-dimensional fields of enormous complexity; the Great Mosque at Cordoba and the Taj Mahal are stunning examples. In stark contrast, Islamic and Arabic dress is simple and austere—robes of plain white or black, devoid of pattern or color. Ornaments are minimal. Once again, there is a surprising disparity, again a dramatic field-event relationship.

In the 1920s the Bauhaus advocated an aesthetic of simplicity, economy and functionality, expressed in the axiom "form follows function." Bauhaus designers adapted classical ideals to industrial demands, paving the way for fifty years of spartan, "modern" architecture. It is no mere coincidence that the same era produced some of the most capricious and playful dress of the twentieth century. Today's disco fashions and yesterday's hippie styles are closely related, although opposite, reactions to the same austere, inorganic architectural environment.

The relationship between dress and architectural environment is different in every culture, sometimes characterized by contrast, other times by harmony. In modern cities, dress is replaced by "fashion," indicating a pattern of continuous challenge and change. The problem is not "keeping up with the Joneses" but "standing out" from them, as individuals seek to assert personal identity and social status in the dense, undifferentiated field of the urban environment. It is not surprising that teenage youth, for whom the identity crisis is particularly intense, are often in the vanguard of the latest fashion. Dress is an interface between individual and environment. In general, such relationships, whether observed in old Japan, the Islamic world or modern America, seem to reveal something fundamental about people and the way they perceive and structure their world.

James McNeill Whistler
Portrait of Alma Stanley in "The Street Walker"
Oil on canvas. 252 × 97.1 cm.
Charles Henry Hayden Fund
Courtesy, Museum of Fine Arts, Boston

Masanobu
Kikugoro as Soga no Goro
Woodblock
Courtesy, Museum of Fine Arts, Boston

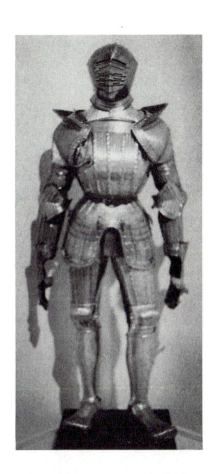

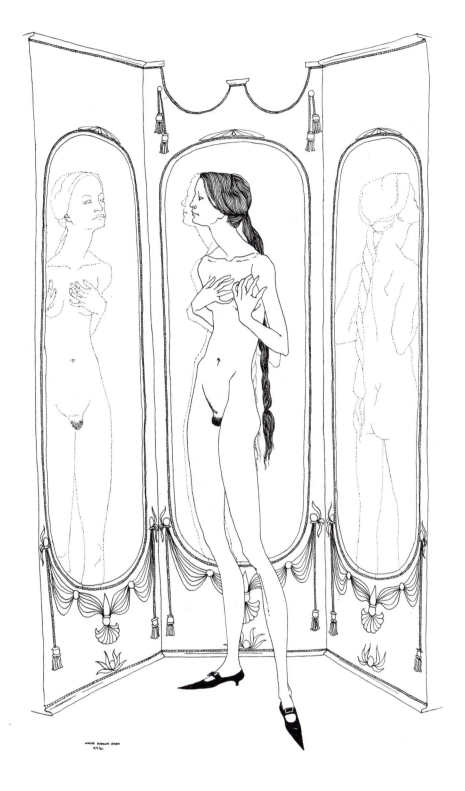

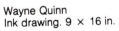

Wayne Quinn
Ink drawing. 9 × 16 in.

Courtesy of the American Museum of Natural History, New York

Herds, Flocks and Fields

Herds are fields. They consist of uniform distributions of similar individuals in space. Just as the bounded field is the simplest form of design, the herd is the simplest form of social organization. Flocks and herds are fields, governed by those laws and dynamics which define all fields.

Fields are unified; in attaining the unity of a field, the herd moves as one. A flock of blackbirds rising suddenly out of the treetops in silent, rhythmic unity is a poetic expression of this oneness.

The anonymous flock or herd is the most ancient form of social organization, or what may be called "society." Konrad Lorenz, well-known author and naturalist, explains that "the flock is determined by the fact that individuals of a species react to each other by attraction and are held together by behavioral patterns which one or more individuals elicit in the others." Schools of fish, flocks of birds or herds of animals are shaped by an elementary force that both attracts individuals of the same species and holds them together. Insect societies—ant colonies or beehives—are shaped by the same elemental force of attraction that coheres herds and schools. This force is as primordial as it sounds, dating back many millions of years before the advent of human beings.

Interestingly enough, the force of attraction between animals increases geometrically as the size of the herd increases. A very large herd, say a thousand members, has many times the force of attraction that a herd half that size has. Moreover, as the size of a herd increases, the value of any single part of it, any individual member, decreases. Lorenz explains that "it is characteristic of the supra-individual community that one individual can be exchanged for any other." If this sounds a little heartless, it is only because of our anthropomorphic way of picturing animals. In fact, herding has its advantages too. In a true herd, all are equal; no member is any better or more important than any other member. There is no ranking order and there is no leader. And herding animals are never lonely. Their reward for anonymity is perpetual union with the whole—the herd.

Courtesy of the American Museum of Natural History, New York

The herd is made up of essentially anonymous members. The larger the herd, the greater the anonymity. Herds preclude not only individual identity but also individuality itself. They are fundamentally impersonal, and so personal bonds cannot be formed. This leads us to a chilly but inescapable conclusion: the peaceable herding creatures of this earth are incapable of friendship.

From here it can be reasoned that small herds are less cohesive than large ones and that yet smaller herds are subject to the formation of break-away subgroups. It is but a small step from these small herds to bands, troops, packs, and prides—social organizations that rarely number more than forty members and often less than thirty. Societies of this size are no longer field-oriented; they are hierarchical—dominance is in full effect, along with ranking order, identity, leadership and, most important, the "personal bond." Konrad Lorenz juxtaposes the "personal bond" to the "anonymous herd"; they are opposites. Bonds are based on personal identity and the value of individuals; herds are based on anonymity and the interchangeability of individuals. This suggests an archetypal field-event relationship in which an archaic field, the "anonymous herd," is juxtaposed to an innovative event, the "personal bond." The rest is history, naturally.

In *African Genesis,* Robert Ardrey builds a strong case for the connection between territory and aggression. His basic premise is that territoriality—the drive to mark, maintain, and defend territory—is a central part of the survival strategy of most animals, and that aggression is the means to that end.

Aggression is a force of repulsion, not attraction. It generates space between individuals, guaranteeing their proper distribution. This distribution is essential for the obvious reason that too many animals in one area quickly exhaust the food supply and bring about the demise of the species. Herds, as we have seen, are shaped by a force of attraction, and it follows logically that they are not aggressive. They need not concern themselves with territory because it is not relevant to the way in which they live. Herds must keep moving. Their very size and numbers make it necessary for them to stay in motion, constantly seeking greener pastures. They are nomadic and migratory. They are concerned with routes rather than territories, and so long as they keep moving, they have no problems with space or spacing. Lorenz writes, "It is typical of flock formation when many individuals travel in close formation in the same direction." In contrast, small bands of animals put less pressure on their environment and so do not have the same urgency to keep moving that herds do. They are more likely to occupy a territory and, according to both Ardrey and Lorenz, defend it with varying degrees of aggressiveness. With smaller numbers comes territoriality, aggression, ranking order, dominance, leadership and, finally, the personal bond. Lorenz explains that "the bond is firmer the more aggressive the particular animal or species is." The wolf, long feared for his legendary ferocity, has come to be admired for his capacity to form lasting bonds. He is known to take a life-long mate and to maintain lasting friendships. It is fitting that the wolf's not-too-distant cousin, the domestic dog, has been humankind's most consistent companion and friend.

Courtesy of the American Museum of Natural History, New York

In nature, dominance usually applies to small or medium-sized groups of individuals, such as a pride of lions or a wolfpack. It is both ineffective and irrelevant in large-scale models like herds. In general, the larger the herd, the less likely it is to display dominance. Herd members do not follow leaders, they follow each other. But how does this apply to human societies?

Like flocks and herds, tribes are field-oriented systems of organization. In general, tribal cultures do not allow the development of either individuality or strong leadership. Both of these are characteristics of literate, Western societies and, although we take them very much for granted, they are quite alien and meaningless in a true tribal social structure. Reporting on his observations of the Mbuti pygmies, anthropologist Colin Turnbull writes, "There are no chiefs or councils, nobody you could even point out as a leader. There are no priests, no judges, no tribal doctors. Someone who seems to have a lot of authority one moment has none the next." Surprising as this may sound at first, it actually makes sense. Tribes are fields. They are expressions of harmony. A strong or outstanding high-contrast event would be disruptive and contrary to the interests of the group. Flocks, herds and tribes find it more advantageous to act "as one" than "for one."

Our population long ago exceeded the modest numbers associated with bands, packs and tribes. We are a super- or supra-herd, numbering hundreds of millions. Theoretically, there are far too many people for dominance to be a viable form of social organization; nature designed dominance for small communities. However, humans have historically managed to befuddle nature; we look like a herd, but we act like a pack.

In the wilderness, herds are not responsive to individual dominance or leadership. In human societies, masses of people are similarly disinclined to be led. We naturally balk at authoritarianism and rule from afar. We refer casually to ourselves as a mass or a public and, like Lorenz's herd, we are essentially anonymous. Our preference is to quietly go about our own business. But governance calls for leadership, and leaders must assert dominance. Throughout history, technology has been called upon to span the abyss between leader and follower, speaker and audience, politician and public. It has made possible centralized authority and central governments. In ages past, technology founded empires; today it shapes nations. Public address systems, mass media and the voting booth all reinforce and perpetuate dominance as naturally as cars promote travel. Technology is tenacious. It enables a few individuals to exert dominance over vast, pacific populations. The resulting hybrid of supra-herd and hierarchical pack represents an innovation that nature never anticipated. In this unmapped social terrain, we are on our own.

Earlier it was said that a herd is a field, and that the bond constitutes an event in that field. By shifting the frame from "herd" to "aggression," we can similarly postulate that aggression is a field in which the personal bond acts as event. If this sounds dramatic, just remember that a century ago Sigmund Freud sought to prove that sex and love were steeped in aggression. Since the bond is extrapolated to mean friendship and love in the human sense, we are not far, then, from the same conclusion.

The genius of human beings is eloquently expressed by the technologies invented throughout history to extend dominance over ever-increasing numbers of individuals. Egyptian papyrus, Roman roads and the United States Senate are all means to extend the authority of a dominant individual or group of individuals. Of course, human society is so complex that one must be wary of generalizations and oversimplifications, but a comparison with animal societies lends support to this idea.

There is an elemental force of attraction between things that are similar or alike. Two similar shapes in a field seem to attract each other as though they were magnetized. A pair of circles, like the moon and sun, tend to converge until they form an eclipse. A pair of deer in a meadow inexorably close the distance between themselves. In social settings, we naturally gravitate towards people with whom we have common interests or backgrounds. We form relationships and personal bonds on the same basis. The reasons for this seem to be obvious, but the archaic nature of this force of attraction is easily overlooked.

In ages past, tribal societies were cohered and shaped by an elemental force which brought together and bonded people with similar needs and goals. The members of the tribe were not just interdependent, they were united; their greatest strength was achieved when they acted as a unit—as one. Indeed, the destiny of one was the destiny of all. Under duress, the tribal bond became even stronger as members sensed their common plight or faced their common enemy. Allegiance to tribe, band or clan was a social imperative; survival depended on it. Ironically, the powerful force of attraction that shaped the tribe also supplied the energy and impetus for aggression. This force, turned outward toward an alien or enemy, fostered behavior which seems atrocious and extreme to the modern sensibility. In the tribal world of "us" and "them," brutality to outsiders was commonplace. Torture was a tradition, part of the overall survival strategy of the tribe. The system was the same for all tribal peoples: the Indian tribes of North and South America, the warlike tribes of Africa—the Masai, Kikuyu or Watusi—and the nomadic Mogul tribes of ancient Asia.

Philip Paratore
Tribal Web
Graphite

Herds, Flocks and Fields

The force of attraction is archaic, yielding the most primitive form of animal society—the herd. Herds are formed by essentially the same force that produced tribal societies among men in the dawn of our social evolution. It has been noted that the force of attraction between animals increases geometrically as the size and density of the herd increases. A large herd has more bonding power than a small one. The attraction also increases as the space between animals decreases; the closer they are, the stronger it gets. This is not a problem as long as the movement of the herd is not restricted and it has free range. However, when range is limited, the herd may become endangered. Such conditions sometimes lead to neurotic or even suicidal behavior; massive "dying off" may occur, naturally thinning out the herd.

The force of attraction in animal and human societies is analogous with the attraction between similar visual elements or events in design. The closer together similar events are, the greater the attraction becomes. Two circles coexist easily in a field if there is plenty of space between them. As that space decreases, they seem to press together with the apparent intention of colliding or uniting. Tension mounts. This may help to explain why, in the art of caricature, close-set eyes appear tense or threatening, while wide-set eyes seem placid. When there are more than two similar events in a field, the attraction between them often leads to the formation of groups. The individual events in such groups tend to relinquish their identity to the whole. Finally, if there are enough of them, they may form a field. The mutual attraction of similar events is a fundamental feature of groups, clans, clusters, cloisters, corporate organizations, tribes, herds, and fields in general.

Paradoxically, there is an equally strong attraction between dissimilar things. Two circles attract each other with a force that is determined by the distance between them. But the same is true for a circle and a triangle. In this case, opposites attract, striving for unity through polar resolution.

Magnetism

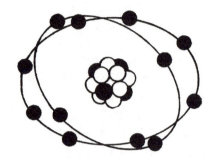

To children, magnetism seems almost magical. Inanimate objects move toward or away from each other as though they had a will of their own. It is the most visible and measurable display of the force of attraction. Science tells us that attraction and repulsion in electrically charged bodies is governed by the following laws:

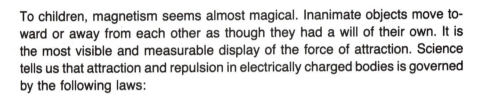

1. **Like-charged bodies repel.**
2. **Unlike-charged bodies attract.**
3. **The force of repulsion or attraction is determined by the distance between the charged bodies.**

Any inquiry into magnetism leads us eventually to the atom. An atom has a nucleus made of protons and neutrons. The protons have a positive charge, the neutrons have no charge. A ring (or rings) of electrons orbit the nucleus; these have a negative charge. Because most atoms have the same number of protons and electrons, they are electrically neutral; they are neither negatively nor positively charged. According to the laws stated above, a positively charged proton will repel another proton but will attract a negatively charged electron. In the atom, the attraction between protons and electrons is limited by the high-speed movement of the electrons as they orbit the nucleus, which propels them outward, away from the nucleus. Without this stabilizing counterforce, electrons could be drawn into the nucleus by the powerful force of attraction. Interestingly enough, it is also movement that preserves the integrity of the herd, as animals are drawn together by an analogous force of attraction.

Scientists can measure magnetic forces with precision. They have found that unlike-charged bodies attract each other with a force that is geometric. If the distance between the two bodies is halved, the force of attraction is quadrupled; if the distance is doubled, the force is one-fourth as great. The attraction between animals in a herd or elements in a design, though less given to measurement, is similarly characterized by a geometric relation, suggesting a rough analogy between animals, art and atoms.

As we said earlier, atoms have equal numbers of protons and electrons. However, electrons sometimes join other atoms or are shared by two atoms, resulting in a "chemical bond." When this happens, an atom may be left with an unequal number of protons and electrons; thus it acquires an electrical charge, depending on whether it has lost or gained an electron. Such charged atoms are called "ions." Subsequently, ions with opposite charges attract

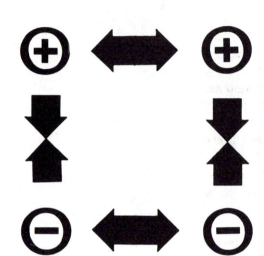

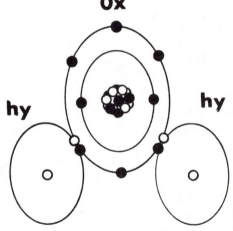

A molecule of water formed by bonding; two atoms of hydrogen share an electron with one atom of oxygen.

each other, forming molecular or chemical compounds. Ions arrange themselves in definite patterns determined by the magnetic forces of attraction and repulsion between them. This is how crystals, for example, come to have distinctive forms. In nature, as in design, appearances are often shaped by unseen forces acting in predictable ways according to consistent laws.

Magnetic Fields

Magnetic fields can be found on every level of life, from the smallest atom to the largest star or galaxy. Earth itself may be compared to a giant magnet with a strong magnetic field. It has geomagnetic north and south poles (negative and positive poles), with an axis running roughly through its center. Lines of force, or vectors, bow out from the poles to encircle the earth in a kind of magnetic envelope. Although the cause of this field is not yet completely understood, it is believed to be related to the movement of the liquid outer core over the solid inner core of the earth as it rotates and orbits through space. In general, where there is movement (spins, orbits, vibrations or fluctuations), there is a magnetic field.

Atoms generate magnetic fields in much the same way as orbiting planets. Electrons orbit the atom's nucleus as the earth orbits the sun, generating a magnetic field. The strength of the field is determined by the sum total of the orbits of all the atom's electrons. For example, if an atom has eight electrons (oxygen), five of which orbit clockwise while the remaining three orbit counterclockwise, a magnetic field results based on the difference of two. However, if four electrons orbit in one direction and four in the other, the result is cancellation—no magnetic field at all.

Atoms with electron parity (cancelling orbits) are said to be balanced. They are stable and disinclined to form chemical bonds in the molecule-building process. Moreover, such atoms share some of the characteristics associated with symmetry. On the other hand, imbalanced atoms (those with a majority of electrons orbiting in one direction) are inclined to form bonds with other atoms. These bonds, or atomic relationships, are reminiscent of pictorial field-event relationships and echo our previous discussions of dominance, tension and resolution.

The spin of the electron as it orbits the nucleus also creates a magnetic field. Like the earth, this field has an axis which runs through the electron's center. When a number of electrons spin so that their axes are parallel (in phase, in wave terminology), the magnetic field is reinforced and strengthened; conversely, when their axes are not parallel (out of phase), they neutralize or cancel each other, resulting in no magnetic field. An iron bar becomes magnetized when its atoms are aligned by parallel axes, that is, all of its atoms are spinning in the same direction.

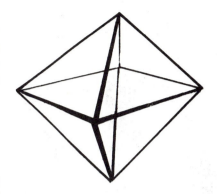

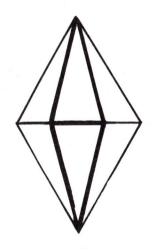

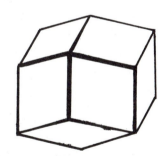

Common crystal forms

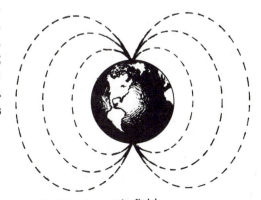

The Earth's magnetic field

Waves

Waves are created whenever energy is added to a field. This is easily demonstrated by throwing a rock into a pond. Concentric waves ripple outward from the point of impact, continuing until the added energy is fully dissipated and the pond is once again calm. Bigger rocks make bigger waves that travel farther, for a longer time. On an infinitely greater scale, stars send light waves radiating across millions of light years of interstellar space before reaching the astronomer's telescope. Light waves from the sun, our own star, warm the earth and provide the energy that makes life possible. Waves are with us, at all times and everywhere.

Waves may be described in terms of the following basic characteristics: crests, troughs, amplitude, wavelength and frequency. A wave, like those made in water, consists of a high point called a crest and a low point called a trough. The strength or amplitude of the wave is measured by the height of its crest; the higher the crest the stronger the wave. The length of a wave or wavelength is measured by the distance between two consecutive crests. And lastly, frequency is measured by the number of waves that pass a given point in one second. Frequency is usually expressed in terms of cycles per second.

Sunlight contains all colors, each of which has its own wavelength and frequency. Blue, for example, has a relatively short wavelength and high frequency; red has a long wavelength and low frequency. As sunlight passes through the earth's atmosphere the shorter wavelengths are partially stopped and scattered, giving the sky its blue appearance.

Unlike light waves, sound waves travel well through any gas, liquid or solid capable of transmitting vibrations. When a tuning fork is struck it vibrates at a specific frequency known as its pitch. Similarly, a piano with its 88 keys may be said to have 88 pitches or frequencies. Low-frequency sounds travel further than high-frequency sounds, but high-frequency sounds such as sirens or whistles have more presence, that is, they tend to be noticed first and most.

Waves are divided into two categories, travelling and standing waves. In the first category are pressure waves, such as those that travel in earth, air or water. Seismographs detect pressure waves that indicate movement in the

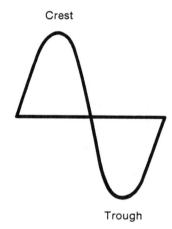

Crest

Trough

earth's crust, just as the human ear detects air pressure waves which we hear as sound. We can also feel low-frequency sound waves with our bodies. The waves created by throwing a rock into a pond or blowing into a saxophone are travelling waves.

In the second category is electromagnetic radiation, a well-known example of which is light. Light travels in standing, or transverse, waves. In *Words and Waves,* A. H. Beck writes, somewhat tentatively, "A fairly adequate definition of a wave is that it is a disturbance moving through a medium." He later adds, "Unfortunately, in the case of electromagnetic waves we must say either that there is no medium or that there is a medium (free space) which exhibits no properties apart from that of transmitting EM waves." Apparently, our understanding of electromagnetic radiation is still being refined and developed. Meanwhile, scientists continue to press their inquiry into waves, particles, packets, quanta, quarks, probability, and infinity, determined to unravel the energy riddles of our universe.

We come now to the main reason for this discussion of waves. It is evident that crests and troughs are opposites; a pair of polar nouns. In our design model, we have postulated that polar adjectives, such as "soft" and "loud," "warm" and "cool" or "bright" and "dull," form essential wholes. Similarly, a crest and a trough form a whole—one wave. However, much more is learned about the dynamics of polar opposition if we posit a second wave. When two waves are identically aligned with each other so that their crests and troughs coincide, they are said to be in phase. In-phase waves that are added together reinforce each other, making bigger, stronger waves. But, should two waves be misaligned so that the trough of one concurs with the crest of the other, the result is mutual cancellation. Returning to our hypothetical pond, if the same rock could magically fall into and rise out of the water at precisely the same time and place, there would be no waves. In this illustration of wave behavior, precisely concurrent opposites cancel or negate each other, vividly demonstrating the dynamism of polarity in nature.

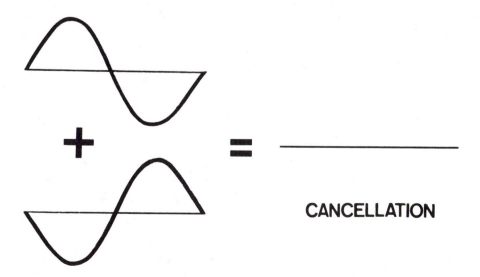

CANCELLATION

PART
VII

Philip Paratore
Elephant Study
Graphite

EXTENSIONS

The Senses: Sight and Sound

The Senses: Sight and Sound

The basic dynamics of vision and audition are surprisingly similar. Both senses are transducers of wave-carried signals or information. Both interact with a limited span of the available frequency range. And both share the same mandate to differentiate and define incoming sensory data. Moreover, our sensorium displays many of the same principles and dynamics we have described in our discussion of design. With these things in mind, let us briefly explore the senses.

Electromagnetic Spectrum

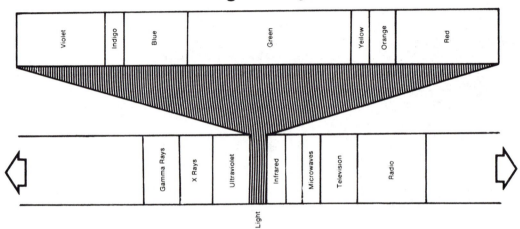

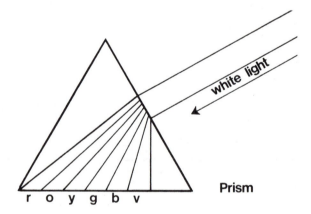

Prism

All radiation, as it is so far known, has a place in the electromagnetic spectrum. Visible light represents a very short span of this spectrum, and it is only within this span that human vision is operative. It is bracketed on the upper end by ultraviolet radiation and on the lower by infrared. Within this limited span of visible light are all the colors of the artist's palette. In the seventeenth century, Newton used a prism to show that the colors of the rainbow are contained in white light. We know today that each color is the result of a remarkably small variation in the frequency of light waves, suggesting a system both simple and discrete.

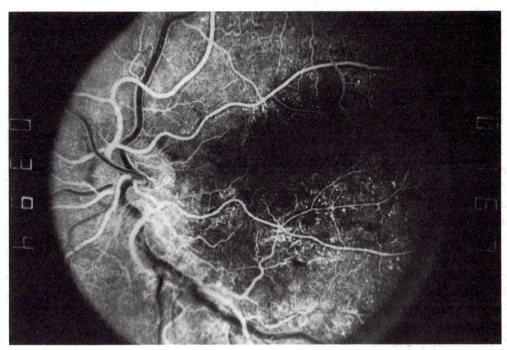

Retina of the human eye

The frequency range of the human ear is about eleven octaves—from 16 to 20,000 cycles per second. But auditory acuity is best around 4,000 cycles per second-the upper octaves of the piano. Sounds below 16 cycles per second are not heard but may be felt as a throb or pulse; they are below the ear's critical fusion threshold. Concert "A" on the piano vibrates at 440 CPS; it may be considered the median for the human voice, indicating the frequency range within which most people normally speak and listen. Interestingly enough, the keyboard synthesizer greatly extends the range of the piano, enabling modern musicians to engage our auditory sense with new vitality.

A common house cat can hear sound frequencies up to 50,000 CPS, more than twice the human limit. Its ears are designed to detect the slightest rustle of rodents in the brush or the faintest flap of bird wings. But the most spectacular ears of all belong to the bat, with an audible range extended to 120,000 CPS. The nocturnal bat lives in an acoustic universe, through which it navigates by *echo-location*. Its ultrasonic cries and shrieks reflect off objects in its "air space," providing it with a continuous-loop feedback system designed for high-speed spatial orientation.

Whales and dolphins employ the same system in navigating the oceans. They are sensitive to sound frequencies of up to 100,000 CPS and their high-pitched cries, whistles and clicks are now thought to be a complex language. Great musicians and composers notwithstanding, human hearing is a modest and limited affair in comparison with the sophisticated hearing of these mammals.

Human vision is more highly developed and sophisticated than animal vision in many ways. Our sensoriums have a distinctly visual bias. So does our culture. We place such high value on seeing that we are surprised that most animals do not see "in color." This includes cats, dogs, horses, deer, elephants and the proverbial red-hating bull. In fact, color perception seems to be a relatively uncommon refinement of vision among mammals. Evidence suggests that it is largely limited to the primates.

If many animals do not share our visual prowess, it is only because they depend on their olfactory and auditory senses more highly. In the animal world, noses and ears are often more important than eyes. The elephant is a dramatic example of this kind of natural sensory preference, with its greatly enlarged ears and extended nose, the result of thousands of years of evolutionary design. It seems that as the elephant's ears grew, its eyes shrank, becoming small and relatively weak. In contrast, predatory birds like hawks and eagles have visual capabilities that are astounding—far superior to those of elephants or humans. But vultures possess the best eyesight of all, largely because of their soaring, scanning lifestyle; they can spot tiny movements or carcasses from miles away. It is not surprising that birds have minimal auditory senses, for their sensory dependence is clearly on their visual powers.

Fish are also visually oriented, extremely sensitive to movement and to color, except those which inhabit deep water not reached by light. However, whales and dolphins have a distinct auditory bias, taking advantage of the fact that sound travels well in water. Research has shown that these aquatic mammals have a hearing range which is much broader and more sensitive than that of humans.

Humans see violet light, but not ultraviolet. However, experiments have shown that honeybees and ants see ultraviolet light and are therefore able to see quite well in conditions that would seem like total darkness to us. On the lower end of the spectrum is infrared radiation. Rattlesnakes have "pit organs" which are sensitive to infrared rays. They use this special sensing ability to locate warm-blooded prey in the dark of night. For this reason, stillness or "freezing" is a hopeless defensive strategy against this predatory snake. In World War II, infrared photography was developed to help locate targets during nighttime aerial reconnaissance missions, providing a technological extension of normal human vision.

Modern technology increasingly extends the reach of our senses in areas that were previously not accessible to the human sensorium. In *Understanding Media,* Marshall McLuhan explains that media are both metaphorical and actual extensions of our senses and that technology is an extension of man himself. If this is true, then as these extensions change so will our description of the world and the universe beyond us. But technology is not the issue here; our underlying message is that all earth's creatures inhabit unique worlds, described and defined by their unique sensoriums. Every species describes a universe—its own.

PART VIII

EXTRAPOLATIONS

Sensory Fields: *a Primary Mode of Perception*

We are born into a world that surrounds us with information in the form of *sensory fields*—undifferentiated masses of sense messages, uniform and homogeneous. As infants, our earliest sensations must be in the context of such fields. The visual world must appear much like a patchwork quilt of meaningless shapes of light and dark, color and texture; the auditory world, an unorchestrated symphony of undifferentiated sounds. No wonder babies sleep so much! In those first months, perhaps the most difficult and strenuous learning of a lifetime occurs. The infant must learn to separate and differentiate "things," to perceive them apart from the sensory field. This process of object (or event) differentiation, so taken for granted by adults, is a pivotal test for the infant; failure here is fatal to learning and growth.

In *The Senses,* Otto Lowenstein describes the experience of adult patients, blind from childhood, who have had their vision restored. He tells of how they are overwhelmed by their first impression of the visual world, unable to make any sense of it. He writes, "one of the most striking facts is that it takes a lot of time and effort before they recognize the objects around them as separate items. At first sight the world looks like a flat extension of meaningless patches of light, dark, and color jumbled up into a quilt work. One by one objects grow out of this chaotic world, and remain unmistakably separate once they have been identified." Evidently, sensory perception is not wholly automatic but is linked to the learning process; in effect, we learn how to see.

If we begin our sensory life by encountering fields, then we grow and learn by recognizing field-event relationships. The adult world is one of separate things, places and spaces. The skills necessary to perceive it that way are slowly developed over the years, and the sensory fields of our infancy are forgotten. Nevertheless, our senses constantly interact with fields, scanning, probing, selecting, focusing—carrying out a program that by now appears to be automatic.

We sometimes revert to our primary mode of sensory perception—scanning sensory fields—without realizing it. In this mode, information is generalized and unfocused; impressions are fleeting, easily forgotten. Our eyes wander, our mind drifts. Travelling in a train across familiar country sometimes induces sensory scanning—we may find ourselves staring out of the window without really seeing anything. We often find this experience relaxing and, indeed, may have trouble keeping our eyes open! Scanning and sleeping are closely related. In the classroom, teachers quickly learn to recognize that "far-away look" in the eyes of youthful students, prompting the admonition to "stop daydreaming and pay attention." Scanning is understandably more common among the young who, after all, are much closer to that early world of sensory fields.

Organization and Learning

One of the basic functions of human intelligence is organizing information. Even on the dullest day our world is full of incoming sensory data, much of it random and disorganized. Perhaps the simplest act of organization is grouping things that are "alike." But almost as elementary is our identification of the thing that stands out, that is "not like the others." In categorizing "likes" and "unlikes," we sort out our world and begin the process of learning. The intellectual tools of decision-making and judgment are slowly forged from these early lessons in organization.

From the very beginning we learn about our world in terms of polar relationships. Our first words come in pairs: "good" and "bad," "yes" and "no," "warm" and "cold." We spend long years expanding this "black and white" vocabulary, but the primary pattern of polar relationships stays the same. It provides the underpinning for our judgmental powers. As we mature we become adept at shading and learn to recognize the many intermediate steps between the poles. Life becomes less stark and less dramatic. We feel more wise. From this humble beginning, intelligence makes its pilgrim's progress.

Time passes. Eventually, we reach a critical point in the learning process; our cultural "program" seems to be complete. We have made all the "normal" connections; our thinking becomes conventional. Repetition and reinforcement displace real learning, yielding less and less insight and limiting intellectual growth. We become "established citizens," set in our ways. Creativity grinds to a halt. However, at this critical juncture a new challenge slowly emerges—to extend the learning process beyond repetitious categorization into the exciting world of speculative thinking, metaphor and conceptual bridge-building. In this new world, ordinary connections, associations and relationships are bypassed in the quest for extraordinary ones. In *The Act of Creation*, Arthur Koestler describes creativity as "the search for hidden similarities." When we discover a connection between ordinarily disparate entities or ideas, we are at the very heart of the creative process. And so a new cycle of learning is begun, one full of challenge and risk, exploration and discovery—a cycle without end, but not without reward.

Our current interest in relationships of polarized adjectives is neither new nor indigenous. Centuries ago, Chinese art critics used a similar approach to make axiomatic statements about the way in which paintings should be designed. In *The Chinese on the Art of Painting*, Osvald Siren includes a passage by the Ch'ing critic Kuo Hsi: "In a picture there may be parts of little importance beside others which should be particularly strong and effective." He later adds, "The paintings of the old masters contain parts which are alive and parts which are dull, parts which are incomplete and parts which are crowded, parts which are delicate and parts which are strong." It is more than coincidental that during the twentieth century, Western cultures began to look more closely at the intuitive yet incisive cognitive modes of the Far East. Like dominance, polar opposition is an ancient program.

"Fast is First"

Basic human learning occurs within a framework of polar relationships. We automatically and instantaneously differentiate information in terms of opposites or poles. There are two outstanding advantages in this cognitive system:

1. **Speed**
2. **Simplicity**

A polar relationship represents a simple arrangement of information. Even with the addition of shading or grading from one pole to the other, it is essentially a simple system. Interestingly enough, simplicity seems to enjoy universal acclaim. In his well-known book, *Art and Visual Perception,* Rudolf Arnheim writes that, "according to the basic law of visual perception, any stimulus pattern tends to be seen in such a way that the resulting structure is as simple as the given conditions permit." He refers to the natural appeal of simplicity, suggesting that great art *looks* simple even when it is highly complex. He cites science's Law of Parsimony which states that, all else being equal, the simplest solution receives preference. Indeed, simplicity seems to be a feature of much that is good in our world. We blame many of our ailments on the complexity of modern society and look nostalgically to the "simple life." But despite its obvious virtues, simplicity is not an end in itself. Its value is explained by an even more basic principle; simple arrangements of information can be comprehended *faster* than complex ones.

In a competitive environment, speed provides a distinct advantage. Nature has evolved a mechanism for snap-judgments, and with good reason, for the survival value of speed is unquestioned. Simple options allow quick response—"yes or no," "fight or flight," "friend or enemy." In the wilderness, life and death are measured in split seconds of reaction time. Slow animals are either very large, like the elephant, or very well protected, like the porcupine; most others depend on speed for survival. Speed requires simplicity, and not the reverse. Nature dictates that fast is first.

Simplicity is a classical ideal of great attractiveness, often associated with balance, restraint and order. But it is not easily defined nor well understood. What is simple in one time and place is often complex in another. Different cultures are likely to have differing ideas about simplicity; a square is a simple shape to a New England carpenter, but may appear complex to an African pygmy who has little experience with straight lines or right angles. In fact, the idea of simplicity tends to be both value-laden and subjective. Simplicity is relative, often a matter of interpretation; speed is more discrete. Although it is not a tenet of classicism, speed is surely a prized ideal of nature.

Tradition

Tradition is environmental. It consists of behavioral patterns, both formal and informal, which are uniform and automatic in a given culture. Historians study traditions from a distant point in time, anthropologists from a distant point in space. But for most people, traditions are not studied; they are lived. They are simply "there" and we can't help but take them for granted. The enduring traditions of ancient Egypt and China were fields to which one paid little conscious attention at the time. They were taken for granted then, just as we take ours for granted today. Indeed, to lavish attention on tradition is to render it forced, frivolous and superficial. The most enduring and significant traditions are those which are least likely to be noticed. Both traditions and environments are fields—uniform, consistent, homogeneous and metaphorically "invisible."

Tradition is naturally conservative. It thrives on consistency and predictability. It fosters conventional or ritual behavior and strives to maintain the status quo. Challenged, it sits pat. Its strategy is to wait and see. At its worst, it meets the threat of change by retrenchment and rejection. Traditional conservatism stays close to home, where it is comfortable and surrounded by the familiar. In the senses, it is cooly automatic; in politics, it is duly autocratic. It is antithetical to art. But, paradoxically, conservatism is essential to creativity; they are as inextricably linked as north and south or hot and cold. Together they form an archetypal field-event relationship.

Innovation

All cultures are characterized chiefly by uniformity. In general, they are field-oriented, and only vary in the degree of uniformity. But how are uniformity and conformity enforced in large, complex cultures such as ours? The answer is, "without really trying." Society naturally fosters conformity by a cultural program which is largely unwritten and unspoken but is nevertheless learned and lived by everyone. Of course, we have rules, laws, charters, constitutions, legislatures and courts, but these in themselves do not account for conventional behavior. Indeed, there is little wisdom in legislating laws for that which occurs naturally and spontaneously. In essence, cultural programs are subliminal.

All innovations impact on culture as events. In varying degrees, they reveal and reshape the field in which they occur. They tend to attract much attention for at least a short while. But a successful innovation is one that finds a useful place within the culture, is accepted and endures. If it endures, it stops being news, loses its novel edge and eventually becomes commonplace. Finally, it merges with the environment or culture and becomes part of the field. This metamorphosis from innovation to convention represents a common pattern of field-event dynamics, applicable to all cultural innovation—artistic, social, scientific or technological.

It is the nature of conventions that they seem always to have been with us. This is most evident in the attitudes of children; they simply can't imagine a world without television, telephones and supermarkets. Adults are not much different. We are all more or less mesmerized by the environments in which we live and the conventions that we live by. The most common conventions—whether they are statements, images or attitudes—are clichés. They represent the stock information of our cultural program. Clichés are deplored by poets and avoided by artists; scientists challenge them, rebellious youths mock them, and politicians flourish on them. Clichés symbolize the conservative leveling tendency of society toward a constant or norm. In many fields—literature, art, science and philosophy—the most extraordinary statements or insights are called "visionary." Visions and clichés are diametric opposites; like innovation and convention, they are two poles of a dynamic, psychosocial continuum.

What is art? How does it function? These are vital questions of great antiquity that are still asked today. As you may have guessed, there are no simple answers. In fact, with each passing decade the definition of art seems to become more elusive. The changing faces of art parade through museums and galleries in a seemingly endless procession. The table of contents in any textbook on the history of modern art tells the story: Expressionism, Impressionism, Cubism, Constructivism, Neo-plasticism, DaDaism, Surrealism, Photorealism, Pop-art, Op-art, Minimal art, Kinetic art, conceptual art and video art are but a few of the diverse directions art has taken in the past one hundred years. Is it possible to coin a definition that would cover such rich variety?

The answer is yes. But we must first agree on the primary function of art—to increase our awareness of environment, the world and life itself. The next question is, exactly how does art accomplish this important-sounding function? Field-event theory helps us to answer this question.

Environments are fields. They are uniform, homogeneous and totally involving. Like fish in water, we are so accustomed to our environments that we are hardly aware of them at all. We naturally take them for granted. Metaphorically speaking, environments are invisible.

Art is an "anti-field." It is an event. Only an event can make a field visible. Art is an event which reveals environment.

The artist, when functioning as an "anti-environmentalist," is capable of perceiving and addressing social and psychic change well in advance of the general population. His or her works, whether they are paintings, poems, films or conceptual schemas, contain the integrals of this advance perception. They are, then, not only a record of occurring or coming change but also a means of filtering timely knowledge of change into the mainstream of society. In this light, the role of the arts and the artist in any modern society is indispensable.

> Art as radar acts as an "early alarm system," as it were, enabling us to discover social and psychic targets in lots of time to prepare to cope with them. This concept of the arts as prophetic contrasts with the popular idea of them as mere self-expression.
>
> Marshall McLuhan

In *The Silent Language,* Edward T. Hall explains that all people are captives of their culture as long as they take their culture for granted. This is also true of environments or fields of any kind. Even our conception of reality is imperceptibly shaped by the environment that surrounds us. What effect does this have on understanding, problem-solving and creativity in general? It is safe to say that it greatly limits awareness and our ability to solve problems; we can't solve them if we can't see them. In this context, art's mission of increasing awareness is an important one indeed.

Art is dynamic. Like gravity, it is easier to explain how it acts than what it is. We experience its effects all the time, but in a thousand different ways. There are many forms of art which don't appear in museums, galleries or art books. Where do they fit in? Paintings, pots and postcards, photographs, plastic still-lifes and plaster madonnas, sculpted gardens and garden sculpture, buildings, rubbings and happenings, Michelangelo's David and Norman Rockwell's illustrations of rosy-cheeked Boy Scouts all share the penumbra of what we call "art." Most art is like casual conversation; it is ubiquitous and commonplace and receives little serious attention. It is essentially environmental. It has a high frequency of occurrence and a correspondingly low value. The more environmental art is, the less it is able to fulfill its function of increasing awareness. Far from sharpening awareness, it contributes to the dulling of our senses by repetition and familiarity. It is decorative rather than evocative. Environmental art merges with the field; it ceases to be an event.

Picture an art continuum with two polarities: field and event. Field-oriented art is environmental—familiar, imitative and decorative. Event-oriented art is anti-environmental—unique and evocative. Most art falls somewhere between these two poles. In essence, fine art is anti-environmental; it stands out and apart from its field. It is special and rare, thus highly valued. It is an extraordinary rather than ordinary occurrence. Fine art has "event" status.

Art is defined in terms of a dynamic continuum. The field is the environment; art is the event. But environments are not permanent, rigid structures. Rather, they are a sea of constant synthesis and change. The result is that art is also constantly changing. What seems important, precious and rare today is often meaningless tomorrow. The value and meaning of a work of art is always tied to its environment—its unique time–space frame. This explains why ordinary objects in one time and place become extraordinary *objets d'art* in another. For example, African sculpture, which is "environmental" in Africa, became "anti-environmental" when introduced into nineteenth-century Europe. In its sudden transformation from field to event status, it generated huge amounts of psychic and cultural energy. The impact of this hybrid energy was profound, leading eventually to Cubism. Today, Eskimo art suffers the same fate as all primitive, exotic or tribal art relocated in modern environments. It loses its original identity and gets a new one from its host museum or gallery. It becomes fine art.

Pablo Picasso
Standing Figure
Oil on canvas. 59 × 39½ in.
Juliana Cheney Edwards Collection
Courtesy, Museum of Fine Arts, Boston

Art in our century has contained many surprises. In a witty reversal of field-event roles, Pop-art turned environmental art anti-environmental; everyday objects became art objects. If only for a brief moment, Brillo boxes, Campbell's soup cans, slick ads and giant hamburgers received the kind of quizzical attention usually reserved for fine art. We found ourselves studying, if not always admiring, household objects that normally filled our shopping cart. By manipulating field-event relations, Pop-art made the familiar seem suddenly strange. Conceptual artists work toward increasing our awareness in much the same way. Earthworks and earth-filled galleries, canvas-wrapped seashores and spartan video installations are anti-environmental; they are designed to challenge tacit assumptions about environment, our world and ourselves.

Changing times affect art as dramatically as changing places. Art history shows that styles or aesthetic movements often reappear decades, sometimes centuries later. The terms "rediscovery" and "rebirth" are reserved for this phenomenon, best exemplified by the Italian Renaissance. In a similar way, the current rage for antiques shows how shifting time frames can lend novel significance to the mundane.

Dolly Darlene
Campbell's Soup Can
Mixed media sculpture

Dolly Darlene
Graphite

Finally, a note on the art of books. A book is a form; it is a frame and also a field. Whenever information of any kind—photographs, drawings, paintings, poems, narration, numerical data—is introduced into a field, it is instantaneously reshaped and renewed. The resulting hybrid acquires a new identity and sense of meaningfulness—not necessarily better or worse—just different; a last reminder that even our most highly regarded forms are essentially fields and are likely to be taken for granted. However, their effect on both information and communication is profound; meaning is always shaped by the field in which it is perceived. The challenge to our awareness is ever-present.

In summary, field-event relationships are in a continuous state of synthesis. Fields confer meaning and value on events; events reveal and reshape fields. It is a dynamic, creative synthesis, defying traditional notions of universality and timelessness. For like nature itself, art involves a process of perpetual challenge, change and, finally, chance.

The Beginning

It seems appropriate to end this book by calling it a beginning. After all, that's exactly what it is. There are so many possible areas of development and exploration that even years more of research and work would barely touch them.

The scope of field-event theory is broad, almost too broad for one person's mind; its thrust is toward teamwork—interdisciplinary collaboration—a meeting of many minds. It calls for new learning models and a new look at the purposes of education. It challenges the assumption that information leads to permanent, verifiable conclusions; while I write, the very subjects I address are reshaping themselves according to a pervasive pattern of change in field-event relationships. It is an ongoing process. Our institutions of education must be similarly vital and dynamic. It is a question of energy and vigilance, without end; we are always just beginning.

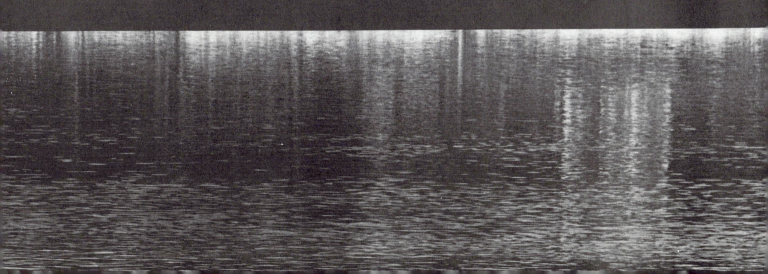

Great accomplishment seems imperfect,
yet it does not outlive its usefulness.
Great fullness seems empty,
yet it cannot be exhausted.

Great straightness seems twisted.
Great intelligence seems stupid.
Great eloquence seems awkward.

Movement overcomes cold.
Stillness overcomes heat.
Stillness and tranquillity set things in order in the universe.

Lao Tsu
Tao Te Ching

GLOSSARY

abstract Designates art or design which emphasizes form and structure apart from recognizable or realistic content.

aesthetics Generally, refers to the appreciation of art and beauty. More specifically, a system or collection of values according to which judgments about art are made.

afterimage The continuance of sensation in a receptor, i.e., the eye, after the originating stimulus has ceased.

ambiguity A state or condition which has two or more possible meanings; indeterminacy. See *tension*.

analogy A comparison which emphasizes similarities between apparently different things. See *metaphor*.

anthropomorphism The practice of superimposing human attributes on nonhuman entities, particularly animals.

archetype An original form or model of something; a highly typical or timeless example.

art Generally, a high order of achievement. Specifically, an extraordinary aesthetic achievement which functions as an event in the context (field) of society.

atmospheric perspective A method for creating the illusion of spatial depth in which things become less defined, lighter in value and bluer in color as they recede in space; sometimes called aerial perspective.

Bauhaus A highly influential school of design founded in Germany in the early twentieth century; emphasized the integration of art and technology.

camouflage A type of natural design in which things are made to blend with their environment.

cathexis The amount of psychic or emotional energy associated with a thing or event.

centrality The organization of information, energy or material around an apparent center. A feature of symmetry.

chemical bond A bond or link between atoms which share an electron.

chiaroscuro The articulation of light and dark in an image; often characterized by high contrast.

classical A descriptive term in art and design which refers to the following characteristics: simplicity, economy, restraint, formal order and rational analysis. Generally, symmetrical, high-definition design.

cliché A frequently occurring expression, idea or image; one that suffers from overuse.

closure Refers to the tendency to make complete wholes out of parts, even when some of the parts are missing or out of place. A tenet of Gestalt psychology.

cognition Refers generally to the process of knowing; modes of acquiring or possessing information.

complementary colors Hues which are opposite and appear as such on the color wheel.

conservatism An ideology or attitude which tends to uphold traditional institutions and conventional behavior.

constancy The eye's tendency to keep the amount of light entering it uniform, i. e., unchanging.

content Subject or subject matter; usually refers to the literal rather than the plastic aspects of an artwork.

contrast The key differentiating agent in sensory perception and design; a method of articulating and defining differences.

convention A customary or socially acceptable practice or precept; juxtaposed to invention and innovation.

creativity A combination of imagination, intelligence and skill that results in original or unique statements, solutions, concepts or images. A mode of behavior characterized by invention and innovation rather than convention and cliché.

crest In wave theory, the peak or high point of a wave. The low point of a wave is called a trough.

critical fusion The phenomenon in which individual units, marks or bits of information merge and blend under certain conditions.

critical fusion density The density at which fusion occurs in spatially oriented phenomena.

critical fusion frequency The frequency at which fusion occurs in temporally oriented phenomena.

crystal A solidified substance made up of symmetrical planes in a three-dimensional arrangement.

definition The sharpness and clarity of an image, particularly in its outline. High-definition images carry more precise, specific information than low-definition images; also applies to nonvisual modes of communication.

depth of field The area which is in focus (depth of focus) in a photograph or through the camera's view-finder.

design Organization; the act of purposeful organization, composition or arrangement.

differentiation The act or process of perceiving and defining things as separate from one another. See *contrast*.

dominance Generally, a system of organization in art and nature; specifically, the capacity to attract and hold attention; a feature of field-event relationships.

dominance factor A characteristic, property or behavior by which dominance may be established.

dot pattern Refers to the halftone screen process used in the print and reproduction industry. Separate dots are calculated to fuse in the viewer's eye to create the illusion of continuous tone or color.

electromagnetic spectrum The range of electromagnetic energy; typically, radio waves to gamma rays; includes visible light.

event A differentiated element of occurrence; an outstanding individual or figure set in contrast to a background or field.

field An area or ground of undifferentiated elements or occurrences; a primary mode of organization based on harmony, consistency and similarity; a set of characteristics which are uniform in time and space.

field-event relationship A relationship consisting of a field and an event; two sets of opposing or differing characteristics, one of which is dominant (the event). A primary mode of organization in perception and design.

field-event theory An interdisciplinary model for the study of design; holds that fields and field-event relationships are primary modes of organizations.

flicker frequency The frequency preceding critical fusion at which sensory acuity is at its lowest; associated with ambiguity and uncertainty.

focal point The dominant event (primary event) in a field.

form The physical or plastic characteristics of a thing or act; the vehicle or support structure for content. In sculpture, it refers to three-dimensional shape or configuration.

frame An actual or apparent border or enclosure which separates information or material from its environment.

frame of reference The field or context in which an observation or judgment is made.

frequency The number of times an event or characteristic is repeated in a given time period. Usually expressed in terms of cycles, i. e., cycles per second.

frequency of occurrence A dynamic principle by which value is often determined, particularly in communication.

geometric In design, a descriptive term which refers to the following characteristics: straight lines, hard edges, angles and an inclination towards measurement.

Gestalt psychology A school of psychology which emerged in Germany early in the twentieth century. It emphasized the role of perception in cognitive processes and developed the figure-ground terminology which is still used today.

ghost dot An optical illusion in which faint dots appear spontaneously at intersections in certain designs.

haiku A traditional form of Japanese poetry consisting of three unrhymed lines of 5, 7 and 5 syllables respectively. Usually a subjective treatment of a transcendental theme.

halftone A reproduction technique using screens to simulate the effect of continuous tone art.

harmony Generally, agreement or concord. Specifically, a mode of organization in which parts blend and merge into unified wholes; a basic characteristic of fields. In music, a technique for arranging groups of different but related tones.

harmony-contrast continuum A graphic concept in which contrast gradually decreases while harmony simultaneously increases; a model of metamorphosis.

hierarchy An organizational system based on dominance and rank order; implicit in field-event relationships.

illusion In general, an appearance which cannot be objectively explained or verified.

innovation Creative rather than imitative activity; often inhibited by convention.

intensity The strength, amplitude or magnitude of a thing or signal. In color, the purity or saturation of hue.

intentional irresolution Design and art in which tension is exploited for expressive purposes. Intentional irresolution is a feature of much so-called modern art, music and drama.

intuition A feeling of knowing which arises spontaneously and cannot be described or explained in logical or rational terms.

ion An atom with an unequal number of protons and electrons, thus possessing an electrical charge.

law of parsimony States that, all else being equal, the simplest solution receives preference.

lens A crystalline or other transparent substance which focuses rays of light as they pass through it. The camera's lens focuses light on the film; the eye's lens focuses light on the retina.

leveling The human tendency to restate, reshape or rearrange ambiguous information or imagery so that it more closely resembles a stock or conventional model.

major matrices An inventory of descriptive terms used to discuss art and design, subdivided into four categories called matrices: (1) conceptual; (2) structural; (3) dynamic; (4) evaluative.

masking When two sounds or signals are simultaneously presented, one of them usually becomes harder to perceive, a phenomenon known as masking in psychology.

mass media Designates media with vast circulations or audiences, such as newspapers and television.

matrix That within which something originates, is articulated or takes form.

media Any material or means by which information is communicated.

medium In general, anything that facilitates communications; in art, a material or process used to express feelings or ideas.

metamorphosis A gradual change in form or function over a given period of time or area of space.

metaphor A poetic expression or image in which one thing or idea is expressed in terms of another, different but related thing or idea.

narrative Designates art that has a literal message; usually associated with realism.

negative shape The shapes or spaces that surround a shape or object when it is projected as positive.

optical illusion A visual illusion generally created by the interplay of two sets of competing, conflicting or contradictory signals.

organic In design, a descriptive term which refers to the following characteristics: curves, soft edges, irregular lines and a disinclination toward measurement.

paradox A statement containing two apparently true but contradictory meanings.

participation mystique The subjective merging of an individual with an experience, usually caused by extreme emotional involvement.

pattern A repetition of three or more events in space.

perception The process of recognizing or identifying something through one of the senses.

peripheral relationships The lowest-ranking relationships in the design hierarchy, i. e., those noticed last and least.

persistence of vision A phrase which refers to the illusion of continuous motion in film projection. The illusion results from the eye's inability to discern gaps between individual film frames.

personal bond A bond or link between two individuals with distinct identities; juxtaposed to the generalized, impersonal bonding of herd members to the herd. Found primarily in aggressive species of animals.

phototropism The natural tendency of plants to face their leaves toward the light.

picture plane The imaginary middle plane from which forms either recede or advance in pictorial space. In flat designs, the frontal or forward-most plane as perceived by the viewer.

plane A real or imagined surface with a specific position in space.

point of view A specific position, actual or apparent, from which an observation or judgment is made. Synonymous with opinion in popular speech.

polarity Refers to the interplay of two opposite or contrary characteristics, such as negative and positive, in a design. A major theme of field-event theory.

polar relationship A relationship based on polarity, opposition or contrast, i. e., black and white or loud and soft.

polar resolution A state or condition in which polarities are unified into wholes; the absence of tension in a polar relationship.

presence The spatial quality of nearness of shapes, colors or objects as perceived by the viewer; a feature of high-definition imagery. In music, the clarity and fidelity of recorded sound.

primary and secondary events Designates rank order of events in a design. See index.

primary relationships The most important or dominant relationships in a design, i. e., those noticed first and most.

principle of unequal division A central principle of field-event theory which recommends avoiding equal or almost equal amounts of opposites in design when the resolution of tension is a goal.

retina The innermost part of the eye upon which images are formed; contains the receptors for vision: rods and cones.

rhythm A repetition of three or more events in time.

rods and cones The eye's sense receptors: rods are responsible for dark adaptation, that is, low-light-level vision; cones are receptors for daylight and color vision.

romantic A descriptive term in art and design which refers to the following characteristics: spontaneity, complexity, movement, subjectivity, integration and emotional involvement. Generally, assymetrical, low-definition design.

scanning Any process in which information is surveyed rapidly and generally; essential in pattern recognition and the apprehension of wholes. In vision, the counterpart of focusing.

secondary relationships Relationships which are subordinate to primary relationships.

semantics The study of meaning, particularly the meanings of words.

sensation The elemental effect of stimuli on a sense organ.

sensory acuity The efficacy or performance level of a sense organ. See *flicker frequency*.

shading The darkening of a color, generally by adding black.

sharpening The tendency to restate, reshape or rearrange ambiguous information or imagery so that it appears less like a stock or conventional model.

simultaneous contrast An optical phenomenon in which a given color spontaneously generates its opposite (complement) under certain conditions.

sound wave A rhythmic alteration of air pressure which results in the impression of sound in the ear.

stereotype A highly generalized or oversimplified model or conception of something; an overused and under-researched idea or image, similar to a cliché.

subjective Refers to a statement or interpretation which is based on the personal feelings and thoughts of the subject; often lacking in objective criteria or common terminology; a low-definition statement or image.

symbol Any mark, sign or object which is used to represent something else; e. g., a country is symbolized by its flag.

symmetry Similarity or equality on either side of a central axis; often associated with classical art.

synesthesia A mental process by which sensation or perception in one sense is translated into another, different sense, e. g., a sight into a sound. A poetic device aimed at enriching and integrating sensory experience.

synthesizer An electronic device capable of producing a vast variety of sounds; sometimes used in conjunction with a keyboard. The main instrument in electronic music.

tatami mat A well proportioned floor mat considered to be a crucial component of traditional Japanese interior design.

tension In design, a state of internal stress caused by uncertainty or ambiguity. The lessening or resolution of tension is a central goal of our perceptual and cognitive processes.

transducer A mechanism or organ which changes energy from one form into another.

tribe A social group of limited size based on a common language, common beliefs and common behavior; often developed around kinship and mutual interdependence. A field-oriented system of organization.

unity A state of oneness and wholeness; the resolution of parts into an organized whole; the general goal of design. See *field-event theory.*

value The lightness or darkness of a color; altered primarily by tinting and shading. In general, the relative worth of something. See *frequency of occurrence.*

values Ideals, criteria or unit measures of worth developed by individuals and cultures; the components of a value system; ethics.

viewing distance The distance at which an image is best viewed and comprehended as a unified whole; usually associated with visual mix but applies to visual experience generally.

visionary A person of extraordinary foresight or insight. Also, one who follows dreams as though they were reality.

visual mix A phenomenon in which colors theoretically mix in the eye of the viewer, rather than on the palette or canvas. See *critical fusion.*

warm and cool color A conventional concept of color temperature: yellow, red and orange are considered warm, blue and violet cool.

wave A form of energy propagation or movement characterized by periodic advances (crests) and retreats (troughs), as in light or sound waves.

wave-length The distance between two given points on a wave; typically, the distance between two crests.

INDEX